Frank Lloyd Wright

DRAWINGS AND PLANS OF FRANK LLOYD WRIGHT
The Early Period (1893–1909)

Dover Publications, Inc.
New York

This Dover edition, first published in 1983, is a republication of the work originally published by
Ernst Wasmuth, Berlin, in 1910 under the title *Ausgeführte Bauten und Entwürfe von Frank Lloyd Wright*.
The present edition omits the German translation of Wright's introductory essay and the German list of
plates. The plate headings have been adapted into English from the original German specially for this
edition, and a glossary of the German terms found in the ground plans has been added. The publisher
gratefully acknowledges the help of Mr. Scott Elliott of the Kelmscott Gallery, 410 South Michigan
Avenue, Chicago, Ill. 60605, in making material available for reproduction.

Library of Congress Cataloging in Publication Data

Wright, Frank Lloyd, 1867–1959.
Drawings and plans of Frank Lloyd Wright.

Originally published as: Ausgeführte Bauten und Entwürfe. Berlin : E. Wasmuth, 1910. German text
omitted.
  1. Wright, Frank Lloyd, 1867–1959.   I. Title.
NA737.W7A4   1983   720′.22′2   82-18229
ISBN-13: 978-0-486-24457-0
ISBN-10: 0-486-24457-1

Manufactured in the United States by Courier Corporation
24457118   2013
www.doverpublications.com

STUDIES AND ☐ ☐ ☐ EXECUTED BUILDINGS BY FRANK LLOYD WRIGHT

FLORENCE, ITALY, June, 1910.

SINCE a previous article, written in an endeavor to state the nature of the faith and practice fashioning this work, I have had the privilege of studying the work of that splendid group of Florentine sculptors and painters and architects, and the sculptor-painters and painter-sculptors, who were also architects: Giotto, Masaccio, Mantegna, Arnolfo, Pisano, Brunelleschi, and Bramante, Sansovino and Angelo.

No line was drawn between the arts and their epoch. Some of the sculpture is good painting; most of the painting is good sculpture; and in both lie the patterns of architecture. Where this confusion is not a blending of these arts, it is as amazing as it is unfortunate. To attempt to classify the works severely as pure painting, pure sculpture, or pure architecture would be quite impossible, if it were desirable for educational purposes. But be this as it may, what these men of Florence absorbed from their Greek, Byzantine and Roman forbears, they bequeathed to Europe as the kernel of the Renaissance; and this, if we deduct the Gothic influence of the Middle Ages, has constituted the soul of the Academic fine arts on the Continent.

From these Italian flames were lighted myriads of French, German and English lights that flourished, flickered feebly for a time, and soon smouldered in the sensuality and extravagance of later periods, until they were extinguished in banal architecture like the Rococo, or in nondescript structures such as the Louvre.

This applies to those buildings which were more or less "professional" embodiments of a striving for the beautiful, those buildings which were "good school" performances, which sought consciously to be beautiful. Nevertheless, here as elsewhere, the true basis for any serious study of the art of architecture is in those indigenous structures, the more humble buildings everywhere, which are to architecture what folk-lore is to literature or folk-songs are to music, and with which architects were seldom concerned. In the aggregate of these lie the traits that make them characteristically German or Italian, French, Dutch, English or Spanish in nature, as the case may be. The traits of these structures are national, of the soil; and, though often slight, their virtue is intimately interrelated with environment and with the habits of life of the people. Their functions are truthfully conceived, and rendered directly with natural feeling. They are always instructive and often beautiful. So, underlying the ambitious and self-conscious blossoms of the human soul, the expressions of "Maryolatry," or adoration of divinity, or cringing to temporal power, there is the love of life which quietly and inevitably finds the right way, and in lovely color, gracious line and harmonious arrangement imparts it untroubled by any burden,—as little concerned with literature or indebted to it as the flower by the wayside that turns its petals upward to the sun is concerned with the farmer who passes in the road or is indebted to him for the geometry of its petals or the mathematics of its structure.

Of this joy in living, there is greater proof in Italy than elsewhere. Buildings, pictures and sculpture seem to be born, like the flowers by the roadside, to sing themselves into being. Approached in the spirit of their conception, they inspire us with the very music of life.

No really Italian building seems ill at ease in Italy. All are happily content with what ornament and color they carry, as naturally as the rocks and trees and garden slopes which are one with them. Wherever the cypress rises, like the touch of a magician's wand, it resolves all into a composition harmonious and complete.

The secret of this ineffable charm would be sought in vain in the rarefied air of scholasticism or pedantic fine art. It lies close to the earth. Like a handful of the moist, sweet earth itself, it is so simple that, to modern minds, trained in intellectual gymnastics, it would seem unrelated to great purposes. It is so close that almost universally it is overlooked.

ALONG the wayside some blossom, with unusually glowing color or prettiness of form, attracts us: held by it, we accept gratefully its perfect loveliness; but, seeking to discover the secret of its charm, we find the blossom, whose more obvious claim first arrests our attention, intimately related to the texture and shape of its foliage; we discover a strange sympathy between the form of the flower and the system upon which the leaves are arranged about the stalk. From this we are led to observe a characteristic habit of growth, and resultant nature of structure, having its first direction and form in the roots hidden in the warm earth, kept moist by the conservative covering of leaf mould. This structure proceeds from the general to the particular in a most inevitable way, arriving at the blossom to proclaim in its lines and form the nature of the structure that bore it. It is an organic thing. Law and order are the basis of its finished grace and beauty; its beauty is the expression of fundamental conditions in line, form and color, true to them, and existing to fulfill them according to design.

We can in no wise prove beauty to be the result of these harmonious internal conditions. That which through the ages appeals to us as beautiful does not ignore in its fibre the elements of law and order. Nor does it take long to establish the fact that no lasting beauty ignores these elements ever present as conditions of its existence. It will appear, from study of the forms or styles which mankind has considered beautiful, that those which live longest are those which in greatest measure fulfill these conditions. That a thing grows is no concern of ours, because the quality of life is beyond us and we are not necessarily concerned with it. Beauty, in its essence, is for us as mysterious as life. All attempts to say what it is, are as foolish as cutting out the head of a drum to find whence comes the sound. But we may study with profit these truths of form and structure, facts of form as related to function, material traits of line determining character, laws of structure inherent in all natural growth. We ourselves are only a product of natural law. These truths, therefore, are in harmony with the essence of our own being, and are perceived by us to be good. We instinctively feel the good, true and beautiful to be essentially one in the last analysis. Within us there is a divine principle of growth to some end; accordingly we select as good whatever is in harmony with this law.

We reach for the light spiritually, as the plant does physically, if we are sound of heart and not sophisticated by our education.

When we perceive a thing to be beautiful, it is because we instinctively recognize the rightness of the thing. This means that we have revealed to us a glimpse of something essentially of the fibre of our own nature. The artist makes this revelation to us through his deeper insight. His power to visualize his conceptions being greater than our own, a flash of truth stimulates us, and we have a vision of harmonies not understood to-day, though perhaps to be to-morrow.

THIS being so, whence came corrupt styles like the Renaissance? From false education, from confusion of the curious with the beautiful. Confounding the sensations awakened by the beautiful with those evoked by things merely curious is a fatal tendency which increases as civilization moves away from nature and founds conventions in ignorance of or defiance of natural law.

The appreciation of beauty on the part of primitive peoples, Mongolian, Indian, Arab, Egyptian, Greek and Goth, was unerring. Because of this their work is coming home to us to-day in another and truer Renaissance, to open our eyes that we may cut away the dead wood and brush aside the accumulated rubbish of centuries of false education. This Renaissance means a return to simple conventions in harmony with nature. Primarily it is a simplifying process. Then, having learned the spiritual lesson that the East has power to teach the West, we may build upon this basis the more highly developed forms our more highly developed life will need.

Nature sought in this way can alone save us from the hopeless confusion of ideas that has resulted in the view that beauty is a matter of caprice, that it is merely a freak of imagination,—to one man divine, to another hideous, to another meaningless. We are familiar with the assertion, that, should a man put eleven stove-pipe hats on top of the cornice of his building and find them beautiful, why then they are beautiful. Yes, perhaps to him; but the only possible conclusion is, that, like the eleven hats on the cornice, he is not beautiful, because beauty to him is utter violation of all the harmonies of any sequence or consequence of his own nature. To find inorganic things of no truth of relation beautiful is but to demonstrate the lack of beauty in oneself and one's unfitness for any office in admin-

A KNOWLEDGE of cause and effect in line, color and form, as found in organic nature, furnishes guide lines within which an artist may sift materials, test motives and direct aims, thus roughly blocking out, at least, the rational basis of his ideas and ideals. Great artists do this by instinct. The thing is felt or divined, by inspiration perhaps, as synthetic analysis of their works will show. The poetry which is prophecy is not a matter to be demonstrated. But what is of great value to the artist in research of this nature is knowledge of those facts of relation, those qualities of line, form and color which are themselves a language of sentiment, and characterize the pine as a pine as distinguished from those determining the willow as a willow: those characteristic traits which the Japanese seize graphically and unerringly reduce to simple geometry: the graphic soul of the thing, as seen in the geometrical analyses of Holkusai. Korin was the conscious master of the essential in whatever he rendered, and his work stands as a convincing revelation of the soul of the thing he portrayed. So it will be found with all great work,--with the paintings of Velasquez and Frans Hals: with Gothic architecture: organic character in all.

By knowledge of nature in this sense alone are these guiding principles to be established. Ideals gained within these limitations are never lost, and an artist may defy his "education." If he is really for nature in this sense, he may be "a rebel against his time and its laws, but never lawless."

The debased periods of the world's art are far removed from any conception of these principles. The Renaissance, Barok, Rococo, the styles of the Louis, are not developed from within. There is little or nothing organic in their nature: they are put on from without. The freedom from the yoke of authority which the Renaissance gave to men was seemingly a great gain: but it served only to bind them senselessly to tradition, and to mar the art of the Middle Ages past repair. One cannot go into the beautiful edifices of this great period without hatred of the Renaissance growing in his soul. It proves itself a most wantonly destructive thing in its hideous perversity. In every land where the Gothic or Byzantine, or the Romanesque, that was close to Byzantine, grew, it is a soulless blight, a warning, a veritable damnation of the beautiful. What lovely things remain, it left to us in spite of its nature or when it was least itself. It was not a development:--it was a disease.

This is why buildings growing in response to actual needs, fitted into environment by people who knew no better than to fit them to it with native feeling,--buildings that grew as folk-lore and folk-song grew,--are better worth study than highly self-conscious academic attempts at the beautiful: academic attempts which the nations seem to possess in common as a gift from Italy, after acknowledging her source of inspiration.

ALL architecture worthy the name is a growth in accord with natural feeling and industrial means to serve actual needs. It cannot be put on from without. There is little beyond sympathy with the spirit creating it and an understanding of the ideals that shaped it that can legitimately be utilized. Any attempt to use forms borrowed from other times and conditions must end as the Renaissance ends,--with total loss of inherent relation to the soul life of the people. It can give us only an extraneous thing in the hands of professors that means little more than a mask for circumstance or a mark of temporal power to those whose lives are burdened, not expressed, by it: the result is a terrible loss to life for which literature can never compensate. Buildings will always remain the most valuable asset in a people's environment, the one most capable of cultural reaction. But until the people have the joy again in architecture as a living art that one sees recorded in buildings of all the truly great periods, so long will architecture remain a dead thing. It will not live again until we break away entirely from adherence to the false ideals of the Renaissance. In that whole movement art was reduced to the level of an expedient. What future has a people content with that? Only that of parasites, feeding on past greatness, and on the road to extinction by some barbarian race with ideals and hungering for their realization in noble concrete form.

IN America we are more betrayed by this condition than the people of older countries, for we have no traditional forms except the accumulated ones of all peoples that do not without sacrifice fit new conditions, and there is in consequence no true reverence for tradition. As some sort of architecture is a necessity, American architects take their pick from the world's stock of "ready-made" architecture, and are most successful when transplanting form for form, line for line, enlarging details by means of lantern slides from photographs of the originals.

This works well. The people are architecturally clothed and sheltered. The modern comforts are smuggled in cleverly, we must admit. But is this architecture? Is it thus tradition molded great styles? In this polyglot tangle of borrowed forms, is there a great spirit that will bring order out of chaos? vitality, unity and greatness out of emptiness and discord?

The ideals of the Renaissance will not, for the Renaissance was inorganic.

A conception of what constitutes an organic architecture will lead to better things once it is planted in the hearts and minds of men whose resource and skill, whose real power, are unquestioned, and who are not obsessed by expedients and forms, the nature and origin of which they have not studied in relation to the spirit that produced them. The nature of these forms is not taught in any vital sense in any of the schools in which architects are trained.

A revival of the Gothic spirit is needed in the art and architecture of modern life: an interpretation of the best traditions we have in the world made with our own methods, not a stupid attempt to fasten their forms upon a life that has outgrown them. Reviving the Gothic spirit does not mean using the forms of Gothic architecture handed down from the Middle Ages. It necessarily means something quite different. The conditions and ideals that fixed the forms of the twelfth are not the conditions and ideals that can truthfully fix the forms of the twentieth century. The spirit that fixed those forms is the spirit that will fix the new forms. Classicists and schools will deny the new forms, and find no "Gothic" in them. It will not much matter. They will be living, doing their work quietly and effectively, until the borrowed garments, cut over to fit by the academies, are cast off, having served only to hide the nakedness of a moment when art became detached, academic, alien to the lives of the people.

A MERICA, more than any other nation, presents a new architectural proposition. Her ideal is democracy, and in democratic spirit her institutions are professedly conceived. This means that she places a life premium upon individuality,--the highest possible development of the individual consistent with a harmonious whole,--believing that a whole benefited by sacrifice of that quality in the individual rightly considered his "individuality" is undeveloped: believing that the whole, to be worthy as a whole, must consist of individual units, great and strong in themselves, not yoked from without in bondage, but united within, with the right to move in unity, each in its own sphere, yet preserving this right to the highest possible degree for all. This means greater individual life and more privacy in life,--concerns which are peculiarly one's own. It means lives lived in greater independence and seclusion, with all toward which an English nobleman aspires, but with absolute unwillingness to pay the price in paternalism and patronage asked of him for the privilege. This dream of freedom, as voiced by the Declaration of Independence, is dear to the heart of every man who has caught the spirit of American institutions: therefore the ideal of every man American in feeling and spirit. Individuality is a national ideal. Where this degenerates into petty individualism, it is but a manifestation of weakness in the human nature, and not a fatal flaw in the ideal.

IN America each man has a peculiar, inalienable right to live in his own house in his own way. He is a pioneer in every right sense of the word. His home environment may face forward, may portray his character, tastes and ideas, if he has any, and every man here has some somewhere about him.

This is a condition at which Englishmen or Europeans, facing toward traditional forms which they are in duty bound to preserve, may well stand aghast. An American is in duty bound to establish traditions in harmony with his ideals, his still unspoiled sites, his industrial opportunities, and industrially he is more completely committed to the machine than any living man. It has given him the things which mean mastery over an uncivilized land,--comfort and resources.

His machine, the tool in which his opportunity lies, can only murder the traditional forms of other peoples and earlier times. He must find new forms, new industrial ideals, or stultify both opportunity and forms. But underneath forms in all ages were certain conditions which determined them. In them all was a human spirit in accord with which they came to be; and where the forms were true forms, they will be found to be organic forms,—an outgrowth, in other words, of conditions of life and work they arose to express. They are beautiful and significant, studied in this relation. They are dead to us, borrowed as they stand.

I have called this feeling for the organic character of form and treatment the Gothic spirit, for it was more completely realized in the forms of that architecture, perhaps, than any other. At least the infinitely varied forms of that architecture are more obviously and literally organic than any other, and the spirit in which they were conceived and wrought was one of absolute integrity of means to ends. In this spirit America will find the forms best suited to her opportunities, her aims and her life.

All the great styles, approached from within, are spiritual treasure houses to architects. Transplanted as forms, they are tombs of a life that has been lived.

THIS ideal of individuality has already ruthlessly worked its way with the lifeless carcasses of the foreign forms it has hawked and flung about in reckless revel that in East, as well as West, amounts to positive riot.

Brown calls loudly for Renaissance, Smith for a French chateau, Jones for an English manor house, McCarthy for an Italian villa, Robinson for Hanseatic, and Hammerstein for Rococo, while the sedately conservative families cling to "old colonial" wedding cakes with demurely conscious superiority. In all this is found the last word of the *inorganic*. The Renaissance ended in this,—a thing absolutely removed from time, place or people; borrowed finery put on hastily, with no more conception of its meaning or character than Titania had of the donkey she caressed. "All a matter of taste," like the hats on the cornice.

A reaction was inevitable.

IT is of this reaction that I feel qualified to speak: for the work illustrated in this volume, with the exception of the work of Louis Sullivan, is the first consistent protest in bricks and mortar against this pitiful waste. It is a serious attempt to formulate some industrial and aesthetic ideals that in a quiet, rational way will help to make a lovely thing of an American's home environment, produced without abuse by his own tools, and dedicated in spirit and letter to him.

The ideals of Ruskin and Morris and the teaching of the Beaux Arts have hitherto prevailed in America, steadily confusing, as well as in some respects revealing to us our opportunities. The American, too, of some old-world culture, disgusted by this state of affairs, and having the beautiful harmony in the architecture of an English village, European rural community, or the grandiloquent planning of Paris in view, has been easily persuaded that the best thing we could do was to adopt some style least foreign to us, stick to it and plant it continually; a parasitic proceeding, and in any case futile. New York is a tribute to the American Beaux Arts so far as surface decoration goes, and underneath a tribute to the American engineer.

Other cities have followed her lead.

Our better-class residences are chiefly tributes to English architecture, cut open inside and embellished to suit; porches and "conveniences" added: the result in most cases a pitiful mongrel. Painfully conscious of their lack of traditions, our get-rich-quick citizens attempt to buy Tradition ready made, and are dragged forward, facing backwards, in attitudes most absurd to those they would emulate, characteristic examples of conspicuous waste.

The point in all this is the fact that revival of the ideals of an organic architecture will have to contend with this rapidly increasing sweep of imported folly. Even the American with some little culture, going contrary to his usual course in other matters, is becoming painfully aware of his inferiority in matters of dress and architecture, and goes abroad for both, to be sure they are correct. Thus assured, he is no longer concerned, and forgets both. That is more characteristic of the Eastern than the Western man. The real American spirit, capable of judging an issue for itself upon its merits, lies in the West and Middle West, where breadth of view, independent thought and a tendency to take common sense into the realm of art, as in life, are more characteristic. It is alone in an atmosphere of this

nature that the Gothic spirit in building can be revived. In this atmosphere, among clients of this type, I have lived and worked.

TAKING common sense into the holy realm of art is a shocking thing and most unpopular in academic circles. It is a species of vulgarity; but some of these questions have become so perplexed, so encrusted by the savants and academies, with layer upon layer of "good school," that their very nature is hidden: approached with common sense, they become childishly simple.

I believe that every matter of artistic import which concerns a building may be put to the common sense of a business man on the right side every time, and thus given a chance at it, he rarely gives a wrong decision. The difficulty found with this man by the Renaissance, when he tries to get inside,—that is, if he does more than merely give the order to "go ahead,"—arises from the fact that the thing has no organic basis to give: there is no good reason for doing anything any particular way rather than another way which can be grasped by him or anybody else: it is all largely a matter of taste. In an organic scheme there are excellent reasons why the thing is as it is, what it is there for, and where it is going. If not, it ought not to go, and as a general thing it doesn't. The people themselves are part and parcel and helpful in producing the organic thing. They can comprehend it and make it theirs, and it is thus the only form of art expression to be considered for a democracy, and, I will go so far as to say, the truest of all forms.

SO I submit that the buildings here illustrated have for the greatest part been conceived and worked in their conclusion in the Gothic spirit in this respect as well as in respect to the tools that produced them, the methods of work behind them, and, finally, in their organic nature considered in themselves. These are limitations, unattractive limitations; but there is no project in the fine arts that is not a problem.

With this idea as a basis, comes another conception of what constitutes a building. The question then arises as to what is style. The problem no longer remains a matter of working in a prescribed style with what variation it may bear without absurdity if the owner happens to be a restless individualist: so this question is not easily answered.

WHAT is style? Every flower has it: every animal has it: every individual worthy the name has it in some degree, no matter how much sandpaper may have done for him. It is a free product,—a by-product, the result of an organic working out of a project in character and in one state of feeling.

An harmonious entity of whatever sort in its entirety cannot fail of style in the best sense.

In matters of art the individual feeling of the creative artist can but give the color of his own likes and dislikes, his own soul to the thing he shapes. He gives his individuality, but will not prevent the building from being characteristic of those it was built to serve, because it necessarily is a solution of conditions they make, and it is made to serve their ends in their own way. In so far as these conditions are peculiar in themselves, or sympathy exists between the clients and the architect, the building will be their building. It will be theirs much more truly than though in ignorant selfhood they had stupidly sought to use means they had not conquered to an end imperfectly foreseen. The architect, then, is their means, their technique and interpreter: the building, an interpretation if he is a true architect in Gothic sense. If he is chiefly concerned in some marvelous result that shall stand as architecture in good form to his credit, the client be damned, why that is a misfortune which is only another species of the unwisdom of his client. This architect is a dangerous man, and there are lots of his kind outside, and some temptations to him inside, the ranks of the Gothic architects. But the man who loves the beautiful, with ideals of organic natures if an artist, is too keenly sensible of the nature of his client as a fundamental condition in his, problem to cast him off, although he may give him something to grow to, something in, which he may be a little ill at ease at the outset.

In this lies temptation to abuses. Where ignorance of the nature of the thing exists or where there is a particular character or preference, it is to a certain extent the duty of an architect to give his client something dated ahead: for he is entrusted by his client with his interests in matters in which, more frequently than not, the client is ignorant. A commission therefore becomes a trust to the architect. Any architect is bound to educate his client to the extent of his true skill and capacity in what he as a professional adviser believes to be fundamentally right. In this there is plenty of leeway for abuse of the client; temptations to sacrifice him in the interest of personal idiosyncrasies, to work along lines instinctively his preference, and therefore easy to him. But in any trust there is chance of failure. This educational relationship between client and architect is more or less to be expected, and of value artistically for the reason that, while the architect is educating the client, the client is educating him. And a certain determining factor in this quality of style is this matter growing out of this relation of architect and client to the work in hand, as well as the more definite elements of construction. This quality of style is a subtle thing, and should remain so, and not to be defined in itself so much as to be regarded as a result of *artistic integrity.*

STYLE, then, if the conditions are consistently and artistically cared for little by little will care for itself. As for working in a nominated style beyond a natural predilection for certain forms, it is unthinkable by the author of any true creative effort.

Given similar conditions, similar tools, similar people, I believe that architects will, with a proper regard for the organic nature of the thing produced, arrive at various results sufficiently harmonious with each other and with great individuality. One might swoop all the Gothic architecture of the world together in a single nation, and mingle it with buildings treated horizontally as they were treated vertically or treated diagonally, buildings and towers with flat roofs, long, low buildings with square openings, mingled with tall buildings with pointed ones, in the bewildering variety of that marvelous architectural manifestation, and harmony in the general ensemble inevitably result: the common chord in all being sufficient to bring them unconsciously into harmonious relation.

IT is with the courage that a conviction of the truth of this point of view has given that the problems in this work have been attempted. In that spirit they have been worked out, with what degree of failure or success no one can know better than I. To be of value to the student they must be approached from within, and not from the viewpoint of the man looking largely at the matter from the depths of the Renaissance. In so far as they are grasped as organic solutions of conditions they exist but to serve, with respect for the limitations imposed by our industrial conditions, and having in themselves a harmony of idea in form and treatment that makes something fairly beautiful of them in relation to life, they will be helpful. Approached from the point of view that seeks characteristic beauty of form and feature as great as that of the Greeks, the Goths or the Japanese, they will be disappointing; and I can only add, it is a little too soon yet to look for such attainment. But the quality of style, in the indefinable sense that it is possessed by any organic thing, that they have. Repose and quiet attitudes they have. Unity of idea, resourceful adaptation of means, will not be found wanting, nor that simplicity of rendering which the machine makes not only imperative but opportune. Although complete, highly developed in detail, they are not.

Self-imposed limitations are in part responsible for this lack of intricate enrichment, and partly the imperfectly developed resources of our industrial system. I believe, too, that much ornament in the old sense is not for us yet: we have lost its significance, and I do not believe in adding enrichment merely for the sake of enrichment. Unless it adds clearness to the enunciation of the theme, it is undesirable, for it is very little understood.

I wish to say, also, what is more to the point,—that, in a structure conceived in the organic sense, the ornamentation is conceived in the very ground plan, and is of the very constitution of the structure. What ornamentation may be found added purely as such in this structure is thus a makeshift or a confession of weakness or failure.

Where the warp and woof of the fabric do not yield sufficient incident or variety, it is seldom patched on. Tenderness has often to be sacrificed to integrity.

It is fair to explain the point, also, which seems to be missed in studies of the work, that in the conception of these structures they are regarded as severe conventions whose chief office is a background or frame for the life within them and about them. They are considered as foils for the foliage and bloom which they are arranged to carry, as well as a distinct chord or contrast, in their severely conventionalized nature, to the profusion of trees and foliage with which their sites abound.

IT is this ideal of an organic working out with normal means to a consistent end that is the salvation of the architect entrusted with liberty. He is really more severely disciplined by this ideal than his brothers of the styles, and less likely to falsify his issue.

So to the schools looking askance at the mixed material entrusted to their charge, thinking to save the nation a terrible infliction of the wayward dreams of mere idiosyncrasies by teaching "the safe course of a good copy," we owe thanks for a conservative attitude, but censure for failure to give to material needed by the nation, constructive ideals that would free from *within* discipline sufficiently, at the same time leaving a chance to work out a real thing in touch with reality with such souls as they have. In other words, they are to be blamed for not inculcating in students the conception of architecture as an organic expression of the nature of a problem, for not teaching them to look to this nature for the elements of its working out in accordance with principles found in natural organisms. Study of the great architecture of the world solely in regard to the spirit that found expression in the forms should go with this. But before all should come the study of the nature of materials, the *nature* of the tools and processes at command, and the *nature* of the thing they are to be called upon to do.

A training of this sort was accorded the great artists of Japan. Although it was not intellectually self-conscious, I have no doubt the apprenticeship of the Middle Ages wrought like results.

German and Austrian art schools are getting back to these ideas. Until the student is taught to approach the beautiful from within, there will be no great living buildings which in the aggregate show the spirit of true architecture.

AN architect, then, in this revived sense, is a man disciplined from within by a conception of the organic nature of his task, knowing his tools and his opportunity, working out his problems with what sense of beauty the gods gave him.

He, disciplined by the very nature of his undertakings, is the only safe man.

To work with him is to find him master of the resources of his tools and materials which may be as complete and in every sense technique in the use of his tools and materials which may be as complete and in every sense as remarkable as a musician's mastery of the resources of his instrument. In no other spirit is this to be acquired in any vital sense, and without it—well—a good copy is the safest thing. If one cannot live an independent life, one may at least become a modest parasite.

SO the forms and the supervisions and refinements of the forms are, perhaps, more elemental in character than has hitherto been the case in highly developed architecture. To be lived with, the ornamental forms of one's environment should be designed to wear well, which means they must have absolute repose and make no especial claim upon attention; to be removed as far from realistic tendencies as a sense of reality can take them. Good colors, soft textures, living materials, the beauty of the materials revealed and utilized in the scheme, these are the means of decoration considered purely as such.

And it is quite impossible to consider the building one thing and its furnishings another, its setting and environment still another. In the spirit in which these buildings are conceived, these are all one thing, to be foreseen and provided for in the nature of the structure. They are all mere structural details of its character and completeness. Heating apparatus, lighting fixtures, the very chairs and tables, cabinets and musical instruments, where practicable, are of the building itself. Nothing of appliances or fixtures is admitted purely as such where circumstances permit the full development of the building scheme.

Floor coverings and hangings are as much a part of the house as the plaster on the walls or the tiles on the roof. This feature of development has given most trouble, and so far is the least satisfactory to myself, because of difficulties inherent in the completeness of conception and execution necessary. To make these elements sufficiently light and graceful and flexible features of an abode requires much more time and thought and money than are usually forthcoming. But it is approached by some later structures more nearly, and in time it will be accomplished. It is still in a comparatively primitive stage of development; yet radiators have disappeared, lighting fixtures are incorporated, floor coverings and hangings are easily made to conform. But chairs and tables and informal articles of use are still at large in most cases, although designed in feeling with the building.

There are no decorations, nor is there place for them as such. The easel picture has no place on the walls. It is regarded as music might be, suited to a mood, and provided for in a recess of the wall if desired, where a door like the cover of a portfolio might be dropped and the particular thing desired studied for a time; left exposed for days, perhaps, to give place to another, or entirely put away by simply closing the wooden portfolio. Great pictures should have their gallery. Oratorio is not performed in a drawing-room. The piano, where possible, should and does disappear in the structure, its key-board or open-work or tracery necessary for sound its only visible feature. The dining table and chairs are easily managed in the architecture of the building. So far this development has progressed.

Alternate extremes of heat and cold, of sun and storm, have also to be considered. The frost goes four feet into the ground in winter; the sun beats fiercely on the roof with almost tropical heat in summer: an umbrageous architecture is almost a necessity, both to shade the building from the sun and protect the walls from freezing and thawing moisture, the most rapidly destructive to buildings of all natural causes. The overhanging eaves, however, leave the house in winter without necessary sun, and this is overcome by the way in which the window groups in certain rooms and exposures are pushed out to the gutter line. The gently sloping roofs grateful to the prairie do not leave large air spaces above the rooms; and so the chimney has grown in dimensions and importance, and in hot weather ventilates at the high parts the circulating-air spaces beneath the roofs, fresh air entering beneath the eaves through openings easily closed in winter.

Conductor pipes, disfiguring down-spouts, particularly where eaves overhang, in this climate freeze and become useless in winter, or burst with results disastrous to the walls; so concrete rain basins are built in the ground beneath the angles of the eaves, and the water drops through open spouts into their concave surfaces, to be conducted to the cistern by underground drain tiles.

ANOTHER modern opportunity is afforded by our effective system of hot water heating. By this means the forms of buildings may be more completely articulated, with light and air on several sides. By keeping the ceilings low, the walls may be opened with series of windows to the outer air, the flowers and trees, the prospects, and one may live as comfortably as formerly, less shut in. Many of the structures carry this principle of articulation of various arts to the point where each has its own individuality completely recognized in plan. The dining-room and kitchen and sleeping-rooms thus become in themselves small buildings, and are grouped together as a whole, as in the Cooley house. It is also possible to spread the buildings, which once in our climate of extremes were a compact box cut into compartments, into a more organic expression, making a house in a garden or in the country the delightful thing in relation to either or both that imagination would have it.

THE horizontal line is the line of domesticity.

The virtue of the horizontal lines is respectfully invoked in these buildings. The inches in height gain tremendous force compared with any practicable spread upon the ground.

To Europeans these buildings on paper seem uninhabitable; but they derive height and air by quite other means, and respect an ancient tradition, the only one here worthy of respect,—the prairie.

In considering the forms and types of these structures, the fact that they are nearly buildings for the prairie should be borne in mind; the gently rolling or level prairies of the Middle West; the great levels where every detail of elevation becomes exaggerated; every tree a tower above the great calm plains of its flowered surfaces as they lie serene beneath a wonderful sweep of sky. The natural tendency of every ill-considered thing is to detach itself and stick out like a sore thumb in surroundings by nature perfectly quiet. All unnecessary heights have for that reason and for other reasons economic been eliminated, and more intimate relation with out-door environment sought to compensate for loss of height.

THE differentiation of a single, certain simple form characterizes the expression of one building. Quite a different form may serve for another; but from one basic idea all the formal elements of design are in each case derived and held together in scale and character. The form chosen may flare outward, opening flower-like to the sky, as in the Thomas house; another, droop to accentuate artistically the weight of the masses; another be non-committal or abruptly emphatic, or its grammar may be deduced from some plant form that has appealed to me, as certain properties in line and form of the sumach were used in the Lawrence house at Springfield; but in every case the motif is adhered to throughout.

In the buildings themselves, in the sense of the whole, there is lacking neither rich-ness nor incident; but these qualities are secured not by applied decoration, they are found in the fashioning of the whole, in which color, too, plays as significant a part as it does in an old Japanese wood block print.

These ideals take the buildings out of school and marry them to the ground; make them intimate expressions or revelations of the interiors; individualize them, regardless of preconceived notions of style. I have tried to make their grammar perfect in its way, and to give their forms and proportions an integrity that will bear study, although few of them can be intelligently studied apart from their environment.

A study of the drawings will show that the buildings presented fall readily into three groups having a family resemblance; the low-pitched hip roofs, heaped together in pyramidal fashion, or presenting quiet, unbroken sky lines; the low roofs with simple pediments countering on long ridges; and those topped with a simple slab. Of the first type, the Winslow, Henderson, Willits, Thomas, Heurtley, Heath, Cheney, Martin, Little, Gridley, Millard, Tomek, Cooley and Westcott houses, the Hillside Home School and the Pettit Memorial Chapel are typical. Of the second type, the Bradley, Hickox, Davenport and Dana houses are typical. Of the third, Atelier for Richard Bock, Unity Church, the concrete house of the *Ladies' Home Journal*, and other designs in process of execution. The Larkin Building is a simple, dignified utterance of a plain, utilitarian type, with sheer brick walls and simple stone copings. The studio is merely an early experiment in "articulation."

A type of structure especially suited to the prairie will be found in the Cooley, Thomas, Heurtley, Tomek and Robie houses, which are virtually one floor arrangements, raised a low story height above the level of the ground. Sleeping-rooms are added where necessary in another story.

There is no excavation for this type except for heating purposes. The ground floor provides all necessary room of this nature, and billiard-rooms, or play-rooms for the children. This plan raises the living-rooms well off the ground, which is often damp, avoids the ordinary damp basement, which, if made a feature of the house, sets it so high above the surface, if it is to be made dry, that, in proportion to the ordinary building operation, it rises like a menace to the peace of the prairie.

It is of course necessary that mural decoration and sculpture in these structures should again take their places as architectural developments conceived to conform to their fabric.

TO thus make of a dwelling place a complete work of art, in itself as expressive and beautiful and more intimately related to life than anything of detached sculpture or painting, lending itself freely and suitably to the individual needs of the dwellers, an harmonious entity, fitting in color, pattern and nature the utilities, and in itself really an expression of them in character,—this is the modern American opportunity. Once founded, this will become a tradition, a vast step in advance of the day when a dwelling was an arrangement of separate rooms, mere chambers to contain aggregations of furniture, the utility comforts not present. An organic entity this, as contrasted with that aggregation: surely a higher ideal of unity, a higher and more intimate working out of the expression of one's life in one's environment. One thing instead of many things; a great thing instead of a collection of smaller ones.

THE drawings, by means of which these buildings are presented here, have been made expressly for this work from colored drawings which were made from time to time as the projects were presented for solution. They merely aim to render the composition in outline and form, and suggest the sentiment of the environment. They are in no sense attempts to treat the subject pictorially, and in some cases fail to convey the idea of the actual building. A certain quality of familiar homelikeness is thus sacrificed in these presentments to a graceful decorative rendering of an idea of an arrangement suggesting, in the originals, a color scheme. Their debt to Japanese ideals, these renderings themselves sufficiently acknowledge.

CHARLES E. ROBERTS, FRANCIS W. LITTLE AND DARWIN D. MARTIN—THREE AMERICAN MEN OF AFFAIRS,—WHO HAVE BELIEVED IN AND BEFRIENDED THIS WORK WHEN NATURAL OPPOSITION FROM WITHOUT AND INHERENT FAULTS WITHIN THREATENED TO MAKE AN END OF IT. WITHOUT THEIR FAITH AND HELP THIS WORK WOULD NEVER HAVE REACHED ITS PRESENT DEVELOPMENT.

FRANK LLOYD WRIGHT.

PLATES

Plate I. House for Mr. W. H. Winslow in River Forest, Illinois, Entrance Detail 16.

Many of the features which have since characterized this work originated in this house. The setting of the basement outside the main walls of the house to form a preparation for the projecting sill courses; the division of the exterior wall surfaces into body and frieze, changing the material above the second story sill line. the wide level eaves, with low sloping roofs; the one massive chimney; and the feeling for contrast between plain wall surface and richly decorated and concentrated masses; the use of the window as a decorative feature in itself; the lines of the building extending into the grounds, the low walls and parterre utilized to associate it with its site. A beautiful elm standing near gave the suggestion for the mass of the building.

Plate II. House for Mrs. Aline Devin. Ground plan and perspective.

A working out of a difficult problem in planning. A house to be built on a fashionable Chicago Drive. lot fifty feet wide extending from the Drive to the lake shore. An arrangement was desired which should respect the thoroughfare and locate the living-rooms toward the lake,—that is, at the rear of the building. The rear outside entrance is screened within the building itself, the library and dining-rooms looking toward the Drive and toward the lake.
An urban character in the exterior. Designed to be executed in brick, stone and tile.

Plate III. Stable of the Winslow house, River Forest. Ground plan and perspective.

Plate IV. Perspective and ground plan of a city dwelling for Isadore Heller, Woodlawn Avenue.

Details of Husser house. Buena Park. Chicago. Built in 1896. Brick walls, tile roofs and plaster frieze

Plate V. Francis Apartments, Forestville Ave. and 32nd St., Chicago.

A characteristic solution of the apartment house problem as it existed in that neighborhood in 1893.

Plate VI. Atelier of Frank Lloyd Wright, Oak Park, Ill.

An early study in articulation—the various functions featured. individualized and grouped.
The working office of the architect.

Plate VII. Bird's eye view of Lexington Terraces.

A solution of the low cost housing problem. typical of the great middle west side of Chicago. The building is an aggregation of 3, 4 and 5-room flats—in two groups. Each group has its own inner court, with central heating, lighting, laundry and janitor service.
A 4-room flat for $20 per month, all included; other flats in proportion.
The entrance to each flat is direct from the outside, all common inside halls and stairs having been avoided, and perfect privacy secured.
All public stairs are located in the open at the angles of the courts, or in recessions of outside wall. Each flat has a rear entrance and rear porch. The plan is the development of the Francisco Terraces built for Mr. E. C. Waller in 1894.

Plate VIII. Perspective of dwelling for Mr. McAfee, Kenilworth, Illinois.

An early design. made about two years after the Winslow house was designed. A suburban dwelling on the lake shore.
Library top lighted: large living-room. light on two sides.
To be executed in brick, stone, and terra cotta with the roof.

Plate IX. Perspective of dwelling for Victor Metzger, Sault Ste. Marie, Michigan.

Study and ground plan of Metzger dwelling.

Plate X. Hillside Home School building.

Built for the Lloyd Jones sisters in 1906.
Exterior walls are native sandstone and solid oak timber construction. Interior throughout framed of exposed solid oak timbers. Walls sandstone below and plastered above.

Plate XI. River Forest Golf Club.

Plate XII. Study for a concrete bank building in a small city.

Illustrating an article contributed to the *Brickbuilder* under the caption. "A Village Bank."

Plate XIII. A typical house intended to form the unit in the group as arranged in the "Quadruple Block Plan."

A new scheme for subdividing property, designed to divide the usual 'American block' into two parts by means of a private way through the center, and to group the houses in squads of four on each half. The houses are so placed that a maximum of privacy, and various advantages of position are made possible.

Plate XIV. Concrete house originally designed for *Ladies' Home Journal.*

A simple house. four sides alike, for sake of simplicity in making forms, with entry added at side, and trellised terrace.
The chimney supports the floors and carries the water from the roof. An insertion of square colored tiles occurs just beneath the soffit of the eaves, certain ones opening for circulation of air in summer. The house may be placed upon the lot in two ways, as shown in schemes A and B.

Plate XV. Perspective view of Thomas P. Hardy house, Racine, Wisconsin.

Plate XVI. Perspective view of the Ullman house.[1]

A further development of the scheme for the Robert Clark house at Peoria.
The dining-room is dropped to the garden level and the covered porch placed above it, both being reached directly from the living-room.
The kitchen is level with the dining-room and the mezzanine stair landings. Study and servants -rooms are level with the covered porch. The bed-room floor is above.

Plate XVII. Perspective of a city dwelling for W. R. Heath, Buffalo, New York. 1903.

Plate XVIII. Suburban dwelling of Frank Thomas, Oak Park, Illinois. 1904.

Plastered on wooden frame. No excavated basement; all rooms above grade. A prairie type.

Plate XIX. Suburban dwelling for Mrs. Martin, Oak Park, Illinois. 1901.

A practical solution of the porch problem.
It is treated here as a semi-detached pavilion placed within the grounds to the south, but not shutting out the sunlight from the living-rooms.
The house is a plastered house, and the eaves are plastic in form.

Plate XX. Dwelling of Arthur Heurtley.

Same type as Thomas house. with living-rooms, kitchen and family bed-rooms on main floor. Two guest-rooms and bath. children's play-room and servants'-room on ground floor. No upper floor.

Plate XXI. Dwelling and garden for W. E. Martin, Oak Park, Illinois.

Plate XXII. Living-room in the residence of Harley Bradley, Kankakee, Illinois.

Two rug patterns.

Plate XXIII. Typical low cost suburban dwelling contributed to the Curtis Publishing Company.

Plate XXIV. Suburban dwelling for Warren F. Hickox, Kankakee, Illinois. 1900.

Plate XXV. Ward W. Willit's ground plan and perspective of villa, Highland Park, Illinois.

A wooden house, plastered outside upon metal lath with cement plaster. Foundation and base-course of cement. Trimmings of wood.

Plate XXVI. Masonry dwelling for Mr. Martin, Buffalo, New York. Adjoining the Martin residence.

A building in the larger Martin group, occupied as a separate residence.
A type of floor plan originated in the Walser house at Austin. The main floor is one large room, with entrance and porch at one side, and stair and kitchen on the other.

Plate XXVII. A plastered house with cement base and wooden trimmings of the open single room type, with alcoved ends, originated in the Warren Hickox house at Kankakee.

Plate XXVIII. Residence of F. W. Little, Peoria, Illinois. 1900.

A residence of cream-colored brick. The plan is as the residence was finally built.
The exterior sketch. the original scheme.

Plate XXIX. House of K. C. De Rhodes at South Bend, Indiana.

A working out of the main floor as a single room. with utility screens. Kitchen and entrance apart. Similar in scheme to Walser. Martin. Henderson and Hickox houses.

Plate XXX. Residence of one-story and basement house of E. H. Cheney, Oak Park, Illinois. 1904.[2]

A one-story brick house set within gardens enclosed by brick walls.
The sleeping-rooms separated from the living-rooms by a corridor.
Heating-room. laundry, store-rooms and servants -rooms in basement.

Plate XXXI. General view of a city dwelling for Mrs. Susan L. Dana, Springfield, Illinois. 1899.

A home designed to accommodate the art collection of its owner and for entertaining extensively, somewhat elaborately worked out in detail.
Fixtures and furnishings designed with the furniture.
It is not entirely new. The old house, which was incorporated in the structure, is outlined by a heavy line on the plan.
The gallery is designed as a gathering place for the artistic activities of the community, and to accommodate the collection made by its owner. It is connected by a covered passage with the house. the passage itself serving as a conservatory.
The hall. dining-room and gallery extend through two stories, and with the ceilings formed in the roof. The terra cotta figure at the entrance was modeled by Richard W. Bock. sculptor.

[1] [Also contains perspective study for the Westcott house.]
[2] [Also contains plan for an artist's house.]

The interior walls are of cream-colored brick closely laid. The woodwork is of freely marked red oak. The sand-finished plaster ceilings are ribbed with wood and stained. Around the dining-room is a decoration of sumac (the plant motif for the decoration of the house proper) and tall flowers, stained in the sand-finished background by George Niedecken.
The furniture and fittings were designed with the buildings.

Plate XXXII. Dwelling of D. D. Martin, Buffalo, New York. 1904.
Reference to the general plan of the Martin house will show certain free standing groups of piers. In the central chamber formed by the piers the radiators are located, and the lighting fixtures are concentrated upon the piers themselves. Bookcases, swinging outward, are placed below between the piers: the open spaces above are utilized as cabinets, and from these the heat passes into the rooms. Fresh air is let into the central chamber through openings between the piers and the bookcases. The radiators are thus made an artistic feature of the architecture.
The Martin house is fireproof, the walls are of brick, floors of reinforced concrete overlaid with ceramic mosaic; roofs tiled. The vitreous brick used in the exterior walls is worked with bronzed joints into the walls and piers of the interior. The brick on these interior surfaces is used in a decorative sense as a mosaic. The woodwork throughout is of fumed white oak. A pergola connects the house with a conservatory, which in turn is connected by means of a covered way with the stable.

Plate XXXIII. Administration building for the Larkin Co. Ground plan and perspective. 1903.
The Larkin Building is one of a large group of factory buildings situated in the factory district of Buffalo. It was built to house the commercial engine of the Larkin Company in light, wholesome, well-ventilated quarters. The smoke, noise and dirt incident to the locality made it imperative that all exterior surfaces be self-cleaning, and the interior be created independently of this environment. The building is a simple working out of certain utilitarian conditions, its exterior a simple cliff of brick whose only 'ornamental' feature is the exterior expression of the central aisle, fashioned by means of the sculptured piers at either end of the main block. The machinery of the various appurtenance systems, pipe shafts incidental thereto, the heating and ventilating air in-takes, and the stairways which serve also as fire-escapes, are quartered in plan and placed outside the building at the four outer corners, so that the entire area might be free for working purposes. These stair chambers are top-lighted. The interior of the main building thus forms a single large room in which the main floors are galleries open to a large central court, which is also lighted from above. All the windows of the various stories or 'galleries' are seven feet above the floor, the space beneath being utilized for steel filing cabinets. The window sash are double, and the building practically sealed to dirt, odor and noise, fresh air being taken high above the ground in shafts extending above the roof surfaces. The interior is executed throughout in vitreous, cream-colored brick, with floor and trimmings of magnesite of the same color. The various features of this trim were all formed within the building itself by means of simple wooden moulds, in most cases being worked directly in place. So the decorative forms were necessarily simple, particularly so as this material becomes hot while setting and expands slightly in the process. The furnishings and fittings are all of steel, and were designed with the structure. The entrance vestibules, from either street and the main lobby, together with the toilet accommodations and rest rooms for employes, are all located in an annex, which intercepts the light from the main office as little as possible. The fifth floor is given to a restaurant for employes, with conservatories in mezzanines over kitchen and bakery at either end, opening in turn to the main roof, all of which together constitutes the recreation ground available for employes. The structure, which is completely fireproof, together with its modern heating, ventilating and appurtenance system, but exclusive of metal fixtures and furnishings, cost but little more than the average high-class fireproof factory building—18 cents per cubic foot. Here, again, most of the critic's architecture has been left out. Therefore the work may have the same claim to consideration as a 'work of art' as an ocean liner, a locomotive or a battle ship.

Plate XXXIV. Country house for C. Thaxter Shaw, Montreal, Canada.
A design for a granite house on the mountain side at Montreal. Approached on either side by drives, passing in front of the house on a terrace arrangement. Entrance through loggia on this terrace to the living-rooms on main floor, which is level with garden at rear and sides. Sleeping-rooms above.
Enclosed garden at front, below terraces.

Plate XXXV. Suburban residence for Mr. Tomek, Riverside, Illinois.
A characteristic 'prairie house,' similar in scheme to the Thomas, Heurtley and Coonley houses.
The plan was later elaborated into the plan of the Robie house.

Plate XXXVI. Exposition building, containing an exhibition-room and lecture-room for the Larkin Co. at the Jamestown Exhibition.
Executed in wood and plaster.

Plate XXXVII. City dwelling of Fred. C. Robie, Woodlawn Ave. and 57th St., Chicago. 1909.
A city dwelling with a south front, built of slender brown bricks, with stone trimmings. Roofs tiled, with copper cornices.

A single room type, similar to Tomek, Coonley and Thomas houses, well open to the south, with balcony and enclosed garden. Sleeping-rooms added in belvedere. Garage connected to house, with servants-rooms over. No excavation except for heater and coal.
A highly developed working out of organic relation between exterior and interior—clean, sweeping lines and low proportions preserving openess and airiness of feature and arrangement throughout.

Plate XXXVIII. "Horse Shoe Inn," Estes Park, Colorado.
A summer hotel or inn on a pine-clad slope of the Colorado mountains. To be built of undressed lumber; the walls sided with wide boards put on horizontally, with battens; stained. The chimneys worked out in rough, flat field stones.

Plate XXXIX. Suburban residence for Mr. Clark, Peoria, Illinois. Perspective and ground plan. 1900.
The dining-room dropped below the living-room, and covered porch above, so that both are reached directly from it by a short flight of stairs. From this side is the outlook over the city and the river. Service is arranged to this porch so that it may be used as a dining-room in summer. It is also connected with the bed-room floor, and may be used as a sleeping porch.

Plate XLa. Workmen's cottages for Mr. E. C. Waller, Chicago, Illinois.
Two stories each and basement.

Plate XLb. Suburban cottage for Miss Grace Fuller, Glencoe, Illinois.

Plate XLI. Pettit Memorial Chapel, Belvidere, Illinois.
A small inexpensive burial chapel at Belvidere, Illinois. A simple, not unhomelike room for services, with shelter at rear and sides to accommodate people waiting for cars.
A memorial tablet and modest fountain characterize it as a memorial to Mr. Pettit.

Plate XLII. River Forest Tennis Club, River Forest, Illinois. 1906.
A simple wooden building set up on posts, built to house the River Forest Tennis Club. Located and planned to afford an outlook over the tennis courts and a good dancing floor, with comfortable ingle nooks.
The walls are of wide boards laid on horizontally, joints covered with battens.

Plate XLIII. A simple wooden house of bungalow type on the edge of a ravine in Glencoe.
Designed to be occupied without servants, although room is provided for them below stairs. The living-room is used as the dining-room in winter. In summer the enclosed veranda is used.

Plate XLIII. A board house for Mr. Stewart at Fresno, California.

Plate XLIII. Sketch for one-story rambling dwelling on the lake shore, beside a deep ravine, at Highland Park, for Mr. Adams.
Plaster and wood.

Plate XLIV. Suburban dwelling for George E. Millard, Highland Park, Illinois.
A simple wooden house in the woods by a Highland Park ravine.

Plate XLV. Cottage for Mrs. Thomas H. Gale, Oak Park, Illinois.
A simple treatment of the small house problem, with flat composition roof.

Plate XLVI. General perspective view of Como Orchard Summer Colony.
Designed to give accommodation to a group of university men owning adjoining orchards and wishing to live near in summer time.
An arrangement of simple wooden cabins with a central club house, where all go for meals, and transients may also be accommodated with rooms.

Plate XLVII. Central club house for the colony.

Plate XLVIIa. Typical cottages, Como Orchard Colony.

Plate XLVIII. Three typical houses for real estate subdivision for Mr. E. C. Waller.
Hip roof, flat roof and gable.

Plate XLIX. Bank and office building for the City National Bank, Mason City, Iowa.
A bank with offices to let above.

Plate L. Cottage for Elizabeth Stone, Glencoe, Illinois.
Design for a summer house in the wood.
Sleeping-rooms, living-room with balcony, and dining-room, which may be opened like a porch, and each separated by small, open, flower-filled courts.

Plate LI. The house of Isabel Roberts in River Forest, Illinois.
A working out for a narrower lot of the plan devised for Wm. Norman Guthrie, Sewanee, Tennessee and afterwards built for Frank T. Baker at Wilmette, Illinois.

Plate LIb. Study for a summer house for Mr. E. C. Waller at Charlevoix, Michigan.

Plate LII. Home for Walter Gerts at Glencoe, Illinois.
A simple gabled residence in a garden behind a wall.
The music-room, on the bed-room floor, the main feature of the house. The roof is doubled, with circulating air spaces between, the upper roof projecting over the ends, the lower over the sides of the building; the rooms extending into the roof space beneath the lower roof.
No excavation. Plan given of lower story on garden level.

Plate LIII. House, pergola and garage for Burton S. Westcott at Springfield, Ohio.[3]
Plastered walls, tile roof, cement base courses and ground work. House of the large living-room type: the necessary privacy for various functions obtained by screens, contrived as bookcases, and seats beside the central fireplace.
In front a tiled terrace, to be covered with awning in summer, and a lily pool, flanked with large cast concrete vases.
The grounds are terraced above the street.

Plate LIV. Concrete flat building at Kenwood for Warren McArthur. Arrangement of three, four and five-room apartments for light housekeeping.
The central court open to the south.

Plate LV. Boathouse for the University of Wisconsin Boat Club.
A shelter for rowing shells on the ground floor, with floating landing piers on either side. The floor above is utilized as a club room, with lockers and bath.

Plate LVI. Dwelling for Mr. and Mrs. Avery Coonley, Riverside, Illinois.
Living-room interior.

Plate LVIa. Dwelling for Mr. and Mrs. Avery Coonley.
Inner perspective of entrance alcove of living-room, and plan showing disposition of furniture.

Plate LVII. Residence of Mr. and Mrs. Avery Coonley.
A one-story house designed for the prairie, with the basement entirely above ground, similar to Thomas, Heurtley and Tomek houses. All rooms, except entrance hall and play-room, are on one floor Each separate function in the house is treated for and by itself, with light and air on three sides, and grouped together as an harmonious whole. The living-room is the pivot of the arrangement, with entrance, play-room and terraces below, level with the ground, forming the main unit of the design. The dining-room forms another unit. The kitchen and servants' quarters are in an independent wing. Family sleeping-rooms form still another unit, and the guest-rooms a pendant wing. Stable and gardener's cottage are grouped together and informally connected by a covered way, which terminates in the gardener's veranda. An arbor crosses the garden to the rear, terminating in the service entrance. The stables, stable yards and gardens are enclosed by plastered walls.

[3][Also contains study for Waller summer house.]

Plate LVIII. Designed for summer residence of Harold McCormick at Lake Forest.
To be cast, window mullions, walls and members in concrete, with overhanging tile roofs.
To be situated on a high bank of Lake Michigan on a projecting point formed by two ravines.
Entrance court toward forest; terraces toward lake. Several porches on either side.
Family bed-rooms in independent wing, with enclosed garden for children; play-house at angle of wall. fountain emptying into head of ravine, which passes beneath the bed-room wing.
Guest-rooms over main rooms. Servants in kitchen wing. Underground corridor connects servants quarters with bed-rooms.

Plan LIX. Summer residence of Harold McCormick, from the lake.

Plate LX. Amusement resort designed to be built at Wolf Lake, Indiana.
Designed to utilize, by means of dredging, a tract of swamp land bordering on a shallow lake in the vicinity of Chicago, as an amusement resort.
The concessions usual to such a project are here screened in a back field by means of uniform entrances constructed on a spacious circular mall.
At the center of the arrangement is the band stand, with a circular tract and field for races and fetes. A covered pergola extends around one side, with seats for onlookers. Back of this a water-court connects the inner lagoon with the lake, so that boats from the cluster may find their way to the lake. Bridges, carrying sale booths, cross this water court, connecting the central field with the mall.
On either side of the central field are casinos, towers, pergolas, boat houses, bathing pavilions, connecting with the adjoining gardens by means of bridges and ways, passing through architectural screens and water courts.
Balloon-carrying lights and colored streamers fixed to flying gaffs are utilized as decorations.

Plate LXI. Dwelling for William Norman Guthrie, Sewanee, Tennessee.

Plate LXII. Atelier in concrete for Richard Bock, sculptor, Oak Park, Illinois.
Designed as a home and workshop for the sculptor. To be located on a lot 50 feet wide by 175 feet deep. A pool occupies the front of the lot.

Plate LXIII. House and temple for Unity Church, Oak Park, Illinois.
A concrete monolith cast in wooden moulds or "forms." After removing the forms the exterior surfaces are washed clean to expose the small gravel aggregate, the finished result in texture and effect being not unlike a coarse granite. The columns, with their decoration, were cast and treated in the same way. The entrance is common to both buildings, and connects them at the center. Both are lighted from above. The roofs are simple reinforced concrete slabs, waterproofed. The auditorium is a frank revival of the old temple form, as better suited to the requirements of a modern congregation than the nave and transept of the cathedral type. The speaker is placed well out in the auditorium, his audience gathered about him in the fashion of a friendly gathering, rather than as fixed in deep ranks, when it was imperative that the priest make himself the cynosure of all eyes. After services the audience moves directly toward the pulpit and out at either side of the auditorium itself. Unity House is designed for the various social activities of the church and for the Sunday school.

Plate LXIV. Facade of Unity Temple.

Glossary of German Terms Found in the Ground Plans

ab: down.
Abhang: slope.
Absatz: landing.
Abzug: sink.
Alkoven: alcoves.
Allee: avenue.
Anfahrt: entrance drive.
Angestellte: employees.
Ankleidezimmer: dressing room.
Anrichtezimmer: pantry.
Arbeitstisch: work table.
Arbeitszimmer: study, workroom.
Atelier: studio.
auf: up.
Aufbewahrungsort: depository.
Ausgang: exit.
Äusseres: outer, exterior.
Ausstellung: exhibition, show, display.

Bach: brook.
Bächlein: rivulet.
Bäckerei: bakery.
Bad: bath, bathroom.
Balkon: balcony.
Balkongeschoss: balcony floor.
Bank: bank, bench.
Baum: tree.
bedeckt: covered.
bedeckte Laube: pergola.
Bedienten: servants.
Berieslungs-Graben: irrigation ditch.
bezeichnet: indicated, marked.
Bibliothek: library.
Bildsäule: statue.
Billardzimmer: billiard room.
Blau: blue.
Blumen: flowers.
Blumenbeet: flowerbed.
Blumengarten: flower garden.
Bogen: arch.
Bogengang: arched arcade.
Bowling Spielplatz: bowling alley.

Brennholz: firewood.
Brücke: bridge.
Brückenbude: booth on a bridge.
Brunnen: fountain.
Bücher: books.
Bücherei: library.
Bücherzimmer: library.
Buchhalter: bookkeeper.
Bude: booth, stall.
Bureau (Büro): office.

Cassirer (Kassierer): cashier.
Chor: choir.
Closet (Kloset): lavatory.
Coje (Koje): stand, stall.

Dach: roof.
Dachgarten: roof garden.
darüber: above.
Deckfenster: skylight.
Diener: servant.
Dienerin: maid.
Dienerinzimmer: maid's room.
Diensthof: servants' yard.
Dienstreppe: service stairs.
Dienst Weg: service way.
Direktor(en): director(s).
Druckerei: print room or shop.
durch: by.

Ecke: corner.
eigenes Zimmer: owner's room.
eingelegt: placed.
Einlage: insertion.
einleitend: preliminary.
Einräumung: concession.
Eintritt: entrance.
Eintrits Halle: entrance hall.
Einzelheit(en): detail(s).
Eis: Ice.
Eltern: parents.
Empfangszimmer: reception room.

Entwurf: sketch.
Entwurfszimmer: drafting room.
Erdengeschoss: ground floor.
erhaben: raised.
erhöht: raised.
Erholungsraum: recreation room.
Esstisch: dining table.
Exhedra: exedra.

Fahreintritt: drive entrance.
Fahrräder: bicycles.
Fahrstuhl: elevator.
Fahrweg: driveway.
farbig: colored.
Fenster: window.
Fensterrahmen: window frame.
Festsaal: banqueting hall.
feuerfest: fireproof.
Feuerraum: furnace.
Frauen: ladies.
Frühstück: breakfast (room).
Fundament: basement.
für: for.
Fuss: foot (feet).
Futter Raum: feed room.

Galerie: gallery.
Gang: passage.
Garderobe: checkroom, wardrobe.
Garten: garden.
Gärtnerhäuschen: gardener's cottage.
Gasse: alley, lane.
Gast-(Schlaf)Zimmer: guest room.
Gedächtnisfeier: memorial service.
Gedächtnisnische: a recess with memorial.
gegen: facing.
Gehege: enclosure.
gelb: yellow.
Geld: money.
gemein: common.
Gerät(e): tool(s).
geschnitten: cut.

Geschoss: floor, story.
Gewölbe: vaulted area.
Gitterwerk: trellis-work, grating.
Glas: glass.
Gold: gold.
Grund: ground.
Grundriss: ground plan.

Halbgrundriss: half ground plan.
Halbkreis: semicircle.
Halle: hall.
Haupteintritt: main entrance.
Hauptgeschoss: main floor.
Haus: house.
Haushälterin: (female) housekeeper.
Hausmeister: caretaker.
Hauswissenschaft: domestic science.
Heizkörper: radiator.
herüber: across.
hinter: rear.
Hof: yard, court.
Höhe: height.
Höhe des Erdbodens: ground-floor level.
höherer Teil: upper portion.
Holz: wood.
Hörsaal: auditorium.
Hühner: chickens.

im Freien: outdoor(s).
in (im): in.
ist: is.

Kamin: chimney, fireplace.
Kanzel: pulpit.
Kassengehilfe: teller.
Keller: cellar.
Kinder: children.
Kinderstube: nursery.
Klavier: piano.
Kleider: clothes (closet).
Kloster: cloister.
Klub-Haus: clubhouse.

Koffer: trunk (room).
Kohlen: coal pile.
Kommis: clerk.
Konzertzimmer: concert room.
Korridor: corridor.
Küche: kitchen.
Kühlraum: refrigeration room.
Kuhstall: cowshed.
Kunstgewerbeklasse(n): applied-arts class(es).
Kunst-Schule: art school.
Kutscher: coaches.

Laboratorium: laboratory.
Laden: shop, store.
Ladentisch: counter.
Lageplan: plan of site.
Landungsbrücke: landing stage, pier, jetty.
Laube: see "bedeckte Laube."
Leinen: linen (closet).
Licht: light.
Lichtschacht: light well.
Lisene(n): pilaster strip(s).

Mädchen: maid.
Männer: men.
Mauer: wall.
Meer: lake.
Metall: metal.
mit: with.
Möbel: furniture.
Mosaik: mosaic.
Musik: music.

Nähstube: sewing room.

ober: upper.

Oberlicht: skylight.
offen: open.
opalescierend: opalescent.
Orgel: organ.
Orgelzimmer: organ loft.

Pavillon: pavilion.
Pfarrer: minister.
Physisches: physics.
Platte(n): plate(s), tile(s).
Privatbureau(s): private office(s).

Querschnitt: cross section.

Rasenplatz: lawn.
Raum: room.
Rednerbühne: speaker's platform.
Rettungsleiter: fire escape.
rot: red.
Ruderboot(e): rowboat(s).

Saal: hall.
Schema: diagram, model, pattern.
Schlaf Veranda: sleeping porch.
Schlafzimmer: bedroom.
Schlucht: ravine.
schräg: slanting, sloping, inclined.
Schrank: closet, locker.
Schrankzimmer: locker room.
Schule: school.
Schüler: student.
Schuppen: shed, garage.
schwimmend: floating.
Sicherheitsgewölbe: safe-deposit vault.
sieben: seven.
sind: there are.
Sitz: seat.

Sitzkasten: window seat, settle.
Sonntagschule: Sunday school.
Speise Tisch: dining table.
Speisezimmer: dining room.
Springbrunnen: fountain.
Stall Hof: stable yard.
Stange(n): mullion(s).
Steinschaft: stone column.
Steinschnitt(e): stone-cutting(s).
Strand: beach, shore.
Strasse: street.
Stuck: stucco.
Stufe: step.
Süd: south.

Tanzsaal: dance hall.
Teich: pool.
Teil: section, portion.
Telefon: telephone.
Telefonzelle: telephone booth.
Tennis Platz: tennis court.
Terrasse: terrace.
tief: deep.
Tisch: table.
Toiletten: toilets.
Treppe: steps, stairs.
Turm: tower.
Turnhalle: gymnasium.
typisch: typical.

über: over.
um: around.
umrändert(e): bordered, edged.
und: and.
unterbrochen: interrupted, broken.
Unterhaltung: maintenance area.

unteriridisch: underground.
untief: shallow.
Urne: urn.

Vereinzimmer: club room.
Ventil: vent, ventilator.
Versammlung: assembly.
versenkt: sunken.
vertieft: sunk, embedded.
Verzierung: decoration.
Vestibul: vestibule.
vier: four.
Viertelgrundriss: quarter ground plan.
Vorbau: porch.
Vorderfront: front.
Vorfahrt: driveway.
Vorrat: store, stock, supply.
Vorzimmer: anteroom.

Wagenremise: coach house.
Wäscherei: laundry room.
Waschraum: toilet.
weiss: white.
Werkstatt: workshop, studio.
Wohnstube: living room.
Wohnung: house, residence, dwelling, living quarters.
Wohnungs Saal: reception room.
Wohnzimmer: living room.

z.: see Zimmer or zu.
Ziegel: brick, tile.
Zimmer: room.
Zirkus: promenade.
zu (zum, zur): to.
zwei: two.
Zwischenstock: mezzanine.

PLATE I(a). House for Mr. W. H. Winslow in River Forest, Illinois. Perspective view.

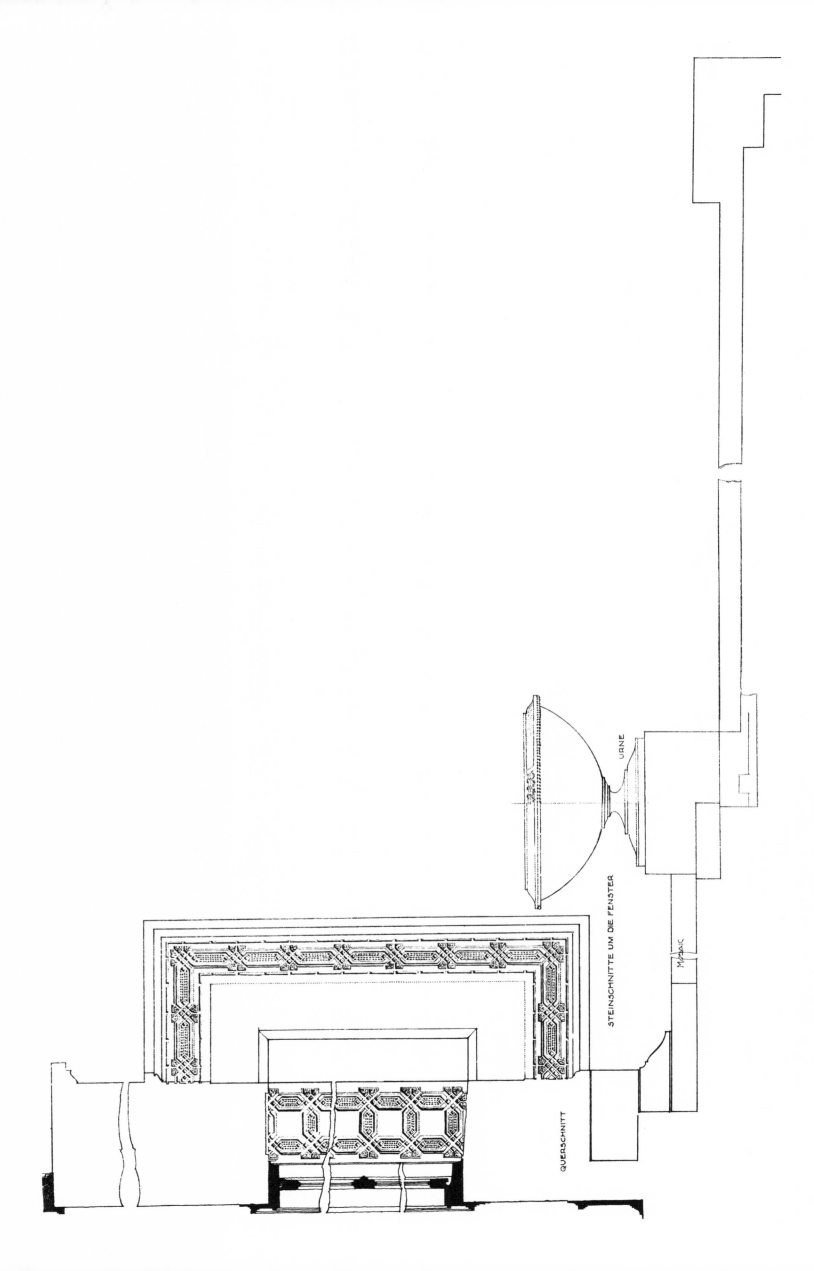

PLATE 1(b). House for Mr. W. H. Winslow in River Forest, Illinois. Entrance detail.

VORDERFRONT

MEER

GERÄTE

KELLER

HEIZKÖRPER

GERÄTE

BILLARDZIMMER

ANFAHRT

FAHRWEG

EINTRITT ZUR KÜCHE

WÄSCHEREI

VORRATSRAUM

FAHRWEG

TERRASSE

SPEISEZIMMER

WOHNZIMMER

BIBLIOTHEK

ARCHITEZIMMER

HALLE

KÜCHE

BEDIENTEN

LAGEPLAN UND GRUNDRISS
DES ERDGESCHOSSES

GRUNDRISS DES
HAUPTGESCHOSSES

DARÜBER SIND
SCHLAFZIMMER

PLATE II. House for Mrs. Aline Devin. Ground plan and perspective view.

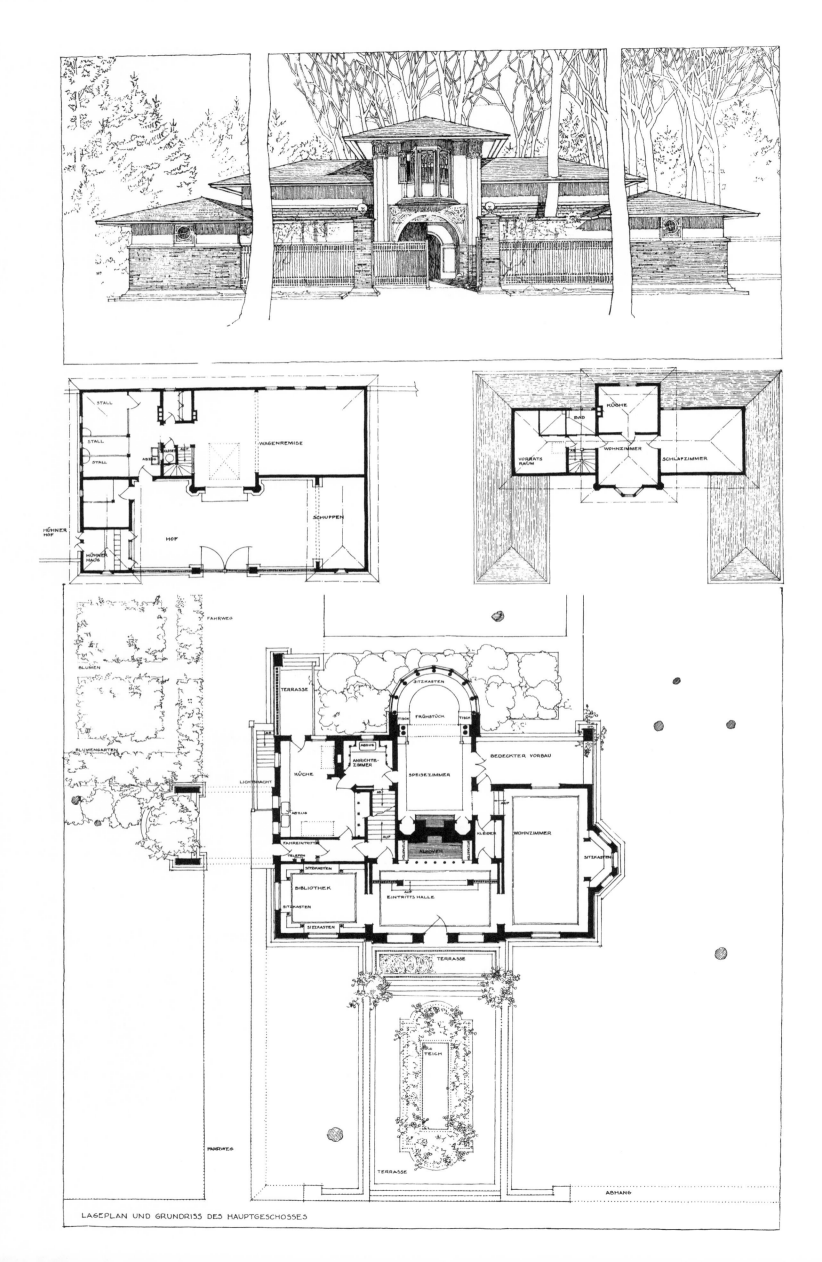

Labels within plans:

STALL
STALL
STALL
WAGENREMISE
CLOSET
ABZUG
SCHUPPEN
HÜHNER HOF
HÜHNER HAUS
HOF

KÜCHE
BAD
VORRATS RAUM
WOHNZIMMER
SCHLAFZIMMER

FAHRWEG
BLUMEN
BLUMENGARTEN
TERRASSE
SITZKASTEN
FRÜHSTÜCK
TISCH
TISCH
LICHTSCHACHT
ABZUG
ANRICHTE-ZIMMER
KÜCHE
SPEISEZIMMER
BEDECKTER VORBAU
ABZUG
KLEIDER
WOHNZIMMER
FAHREINTRITT
TELEFON
SITZKASTEN
ALKOVEN
SITZKASTEN
BIBLIOTHEK
EINTRITTS HALLE
SITZKASTEN
SITZKASTEN
TERRASSE
FAHRWEG
TEICH
TERRASSE
ABHANG

LAGEPLAN UND GRUNDRISS DES HAUPTGESCHOSSES

PLATE III. Stable of the Winslow house, River Forest. Ground plan and perspective view.

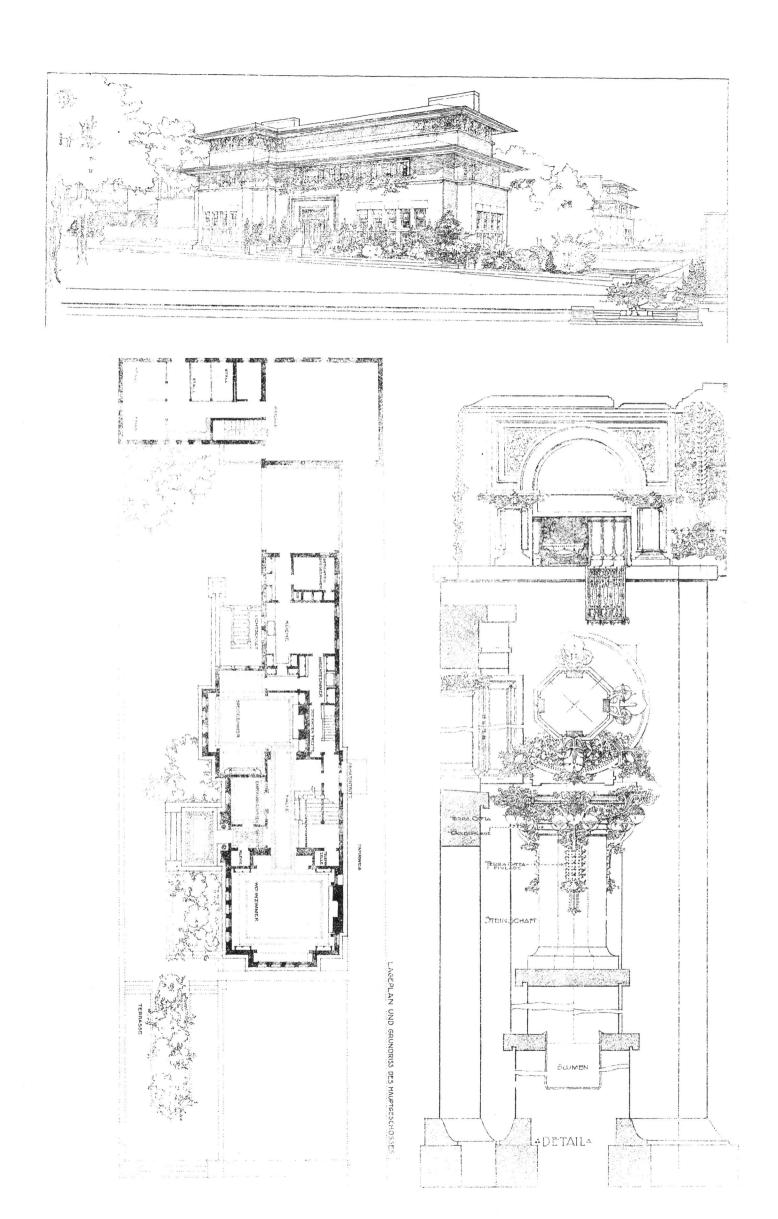

Labels visible on plans: STALL, KÜCHE, ARBEITSZIMMER, EMPFANGSZIMMER, HALLE, WOHNZIMMER, TERRASSE

LAGEPLAN UND GRUNDRISS DES HAUPTGESCHOSSES

Detail labels: BLUMEN, TERRA-COTTA GOLDEINLAGE, TERRA-COTTA EINLAGE, STEINSCHAFT, BLUMEN

·DETAIL·

PLATE IV. Perspective view and ground plan of a city dwelling for Isadore Heller. Woodlawn Avenue.

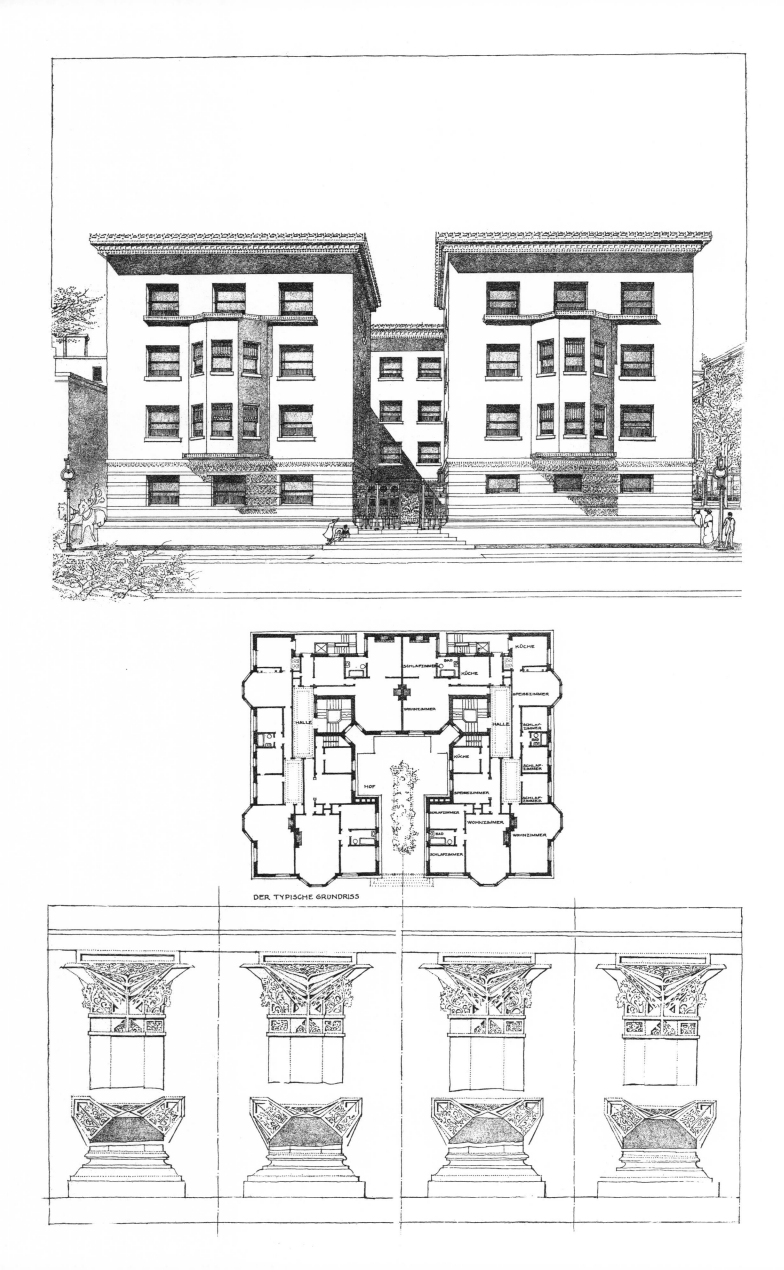

DER TYPISCHE GRUNDRISS

PLATE V. Francis Apartments. Forestville Ave. and 32nd St., Chicago.

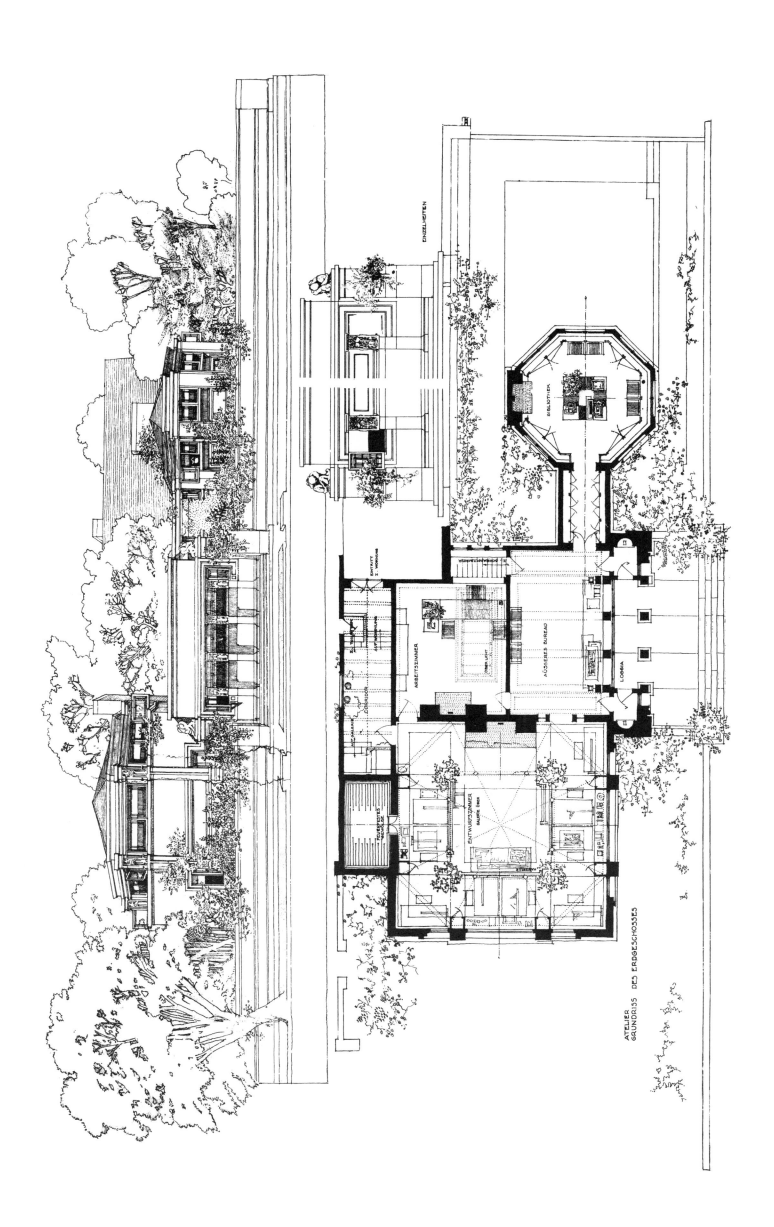

ATELIER
GRUNDRISS DES ERDGESCHOSSES

PLATE VI. Atelier of Frank Lloyd Wright, Oak Park, Ill.

PLATE VII(a). Bird's eye view of Lexington Terraces.

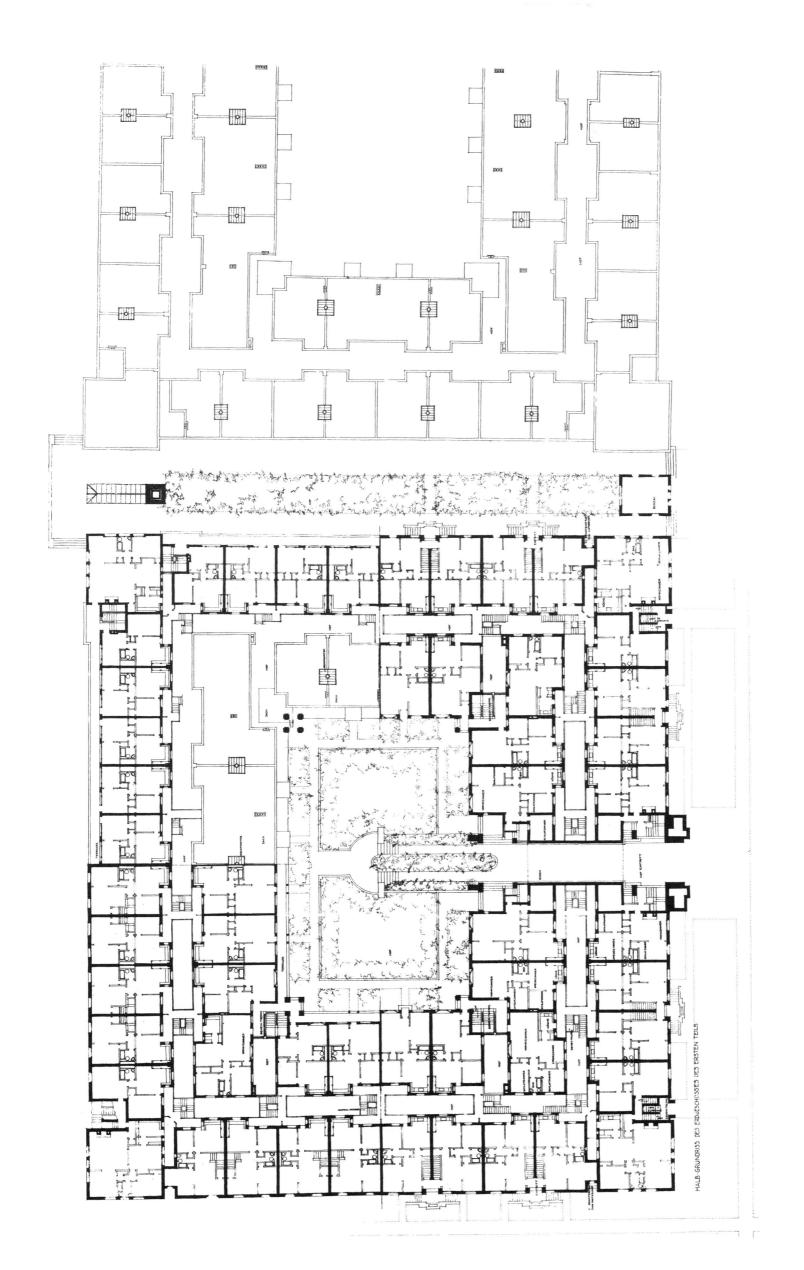

HALB GRUNDRISS DES ERDGESCHOSSES DES ERSTEN TEILS

PLATE VII(b). Lexington Terraces. Ground plan.

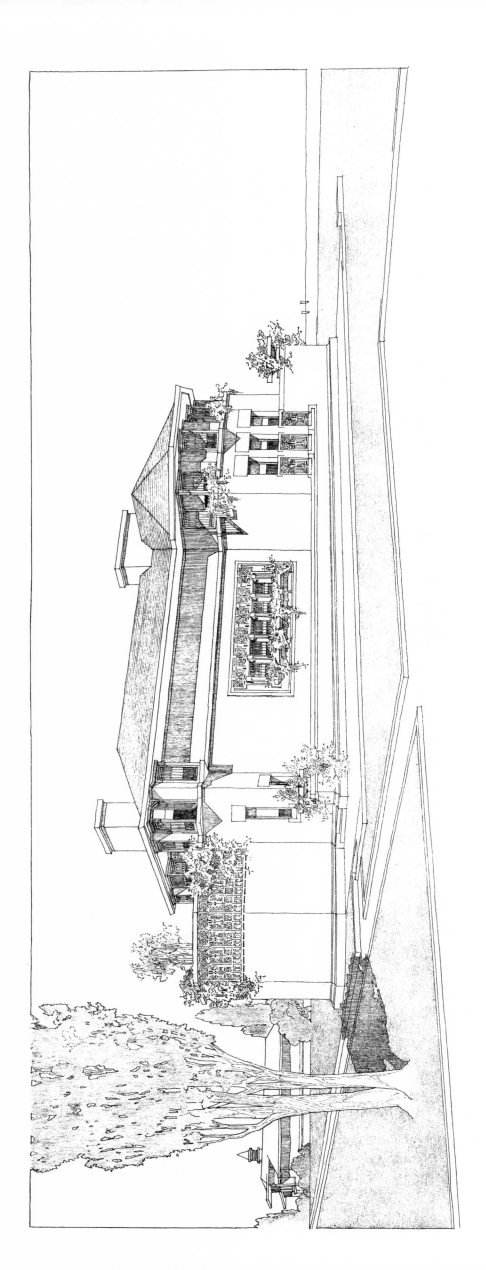

PLATE VIII(a). Perspective view of dwelling for Mr. McAfee, Kenilworth, Ill.

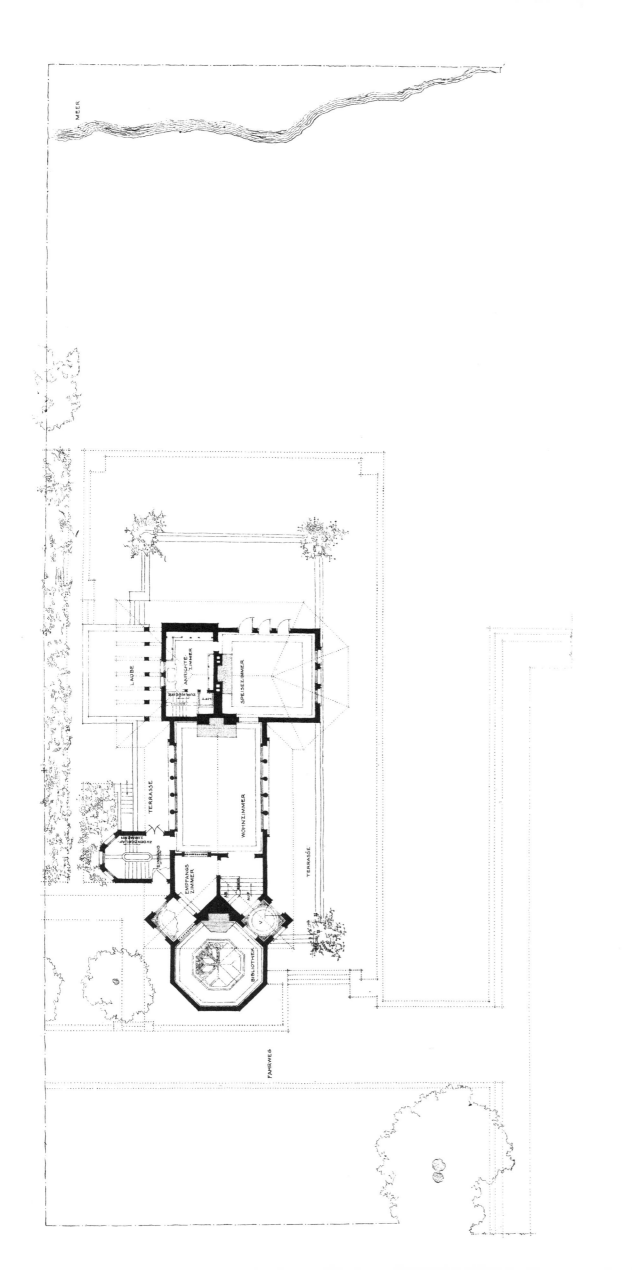

MEER

LAUBE

TERRASSE

ANRICHTE-ZIMMER

SPEISEZIMMER

WOHNZIMMER

TERRASSE

EMPFANGS-ZIMMER

ZUR DIENERSCHAFT

BIBLIOTHEK

FAHRWEG

PLATE VIII(b). Dwelling for Mr. McAfee. Ground plan.

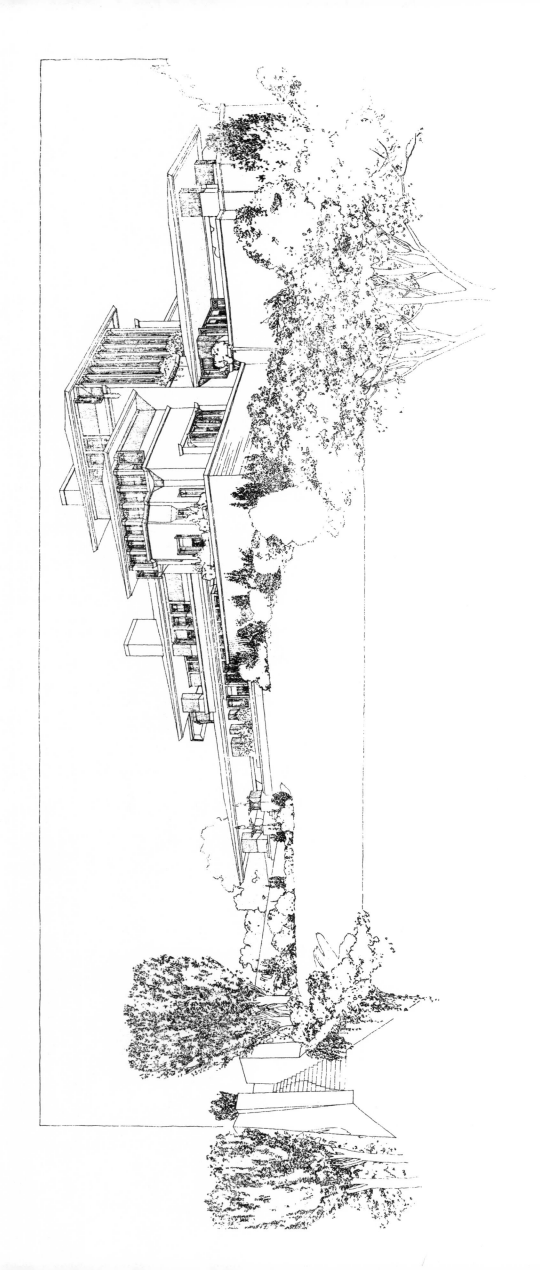

PLATE IX(a). Perspective view of dwelling for Victor Metzger, Sault Ste. Marie, Mich.

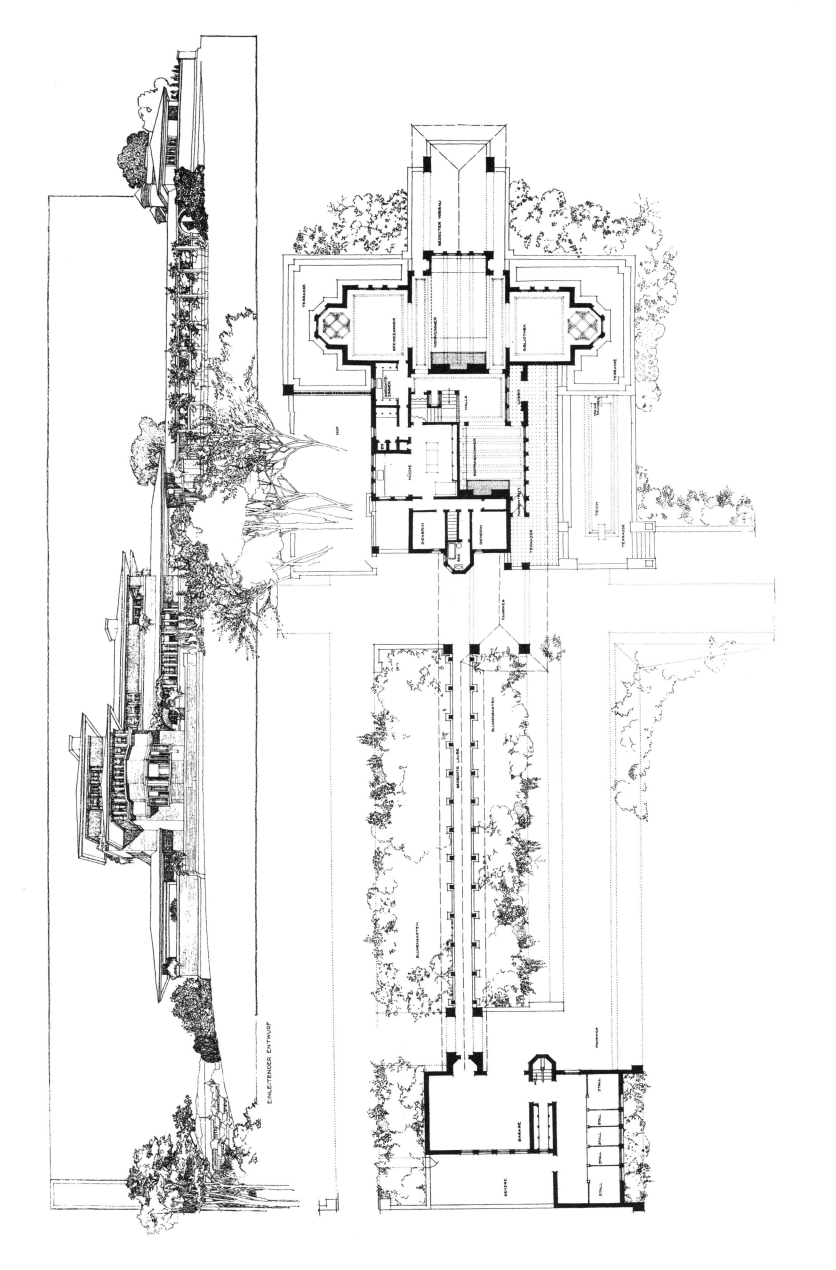

PLATE IX(b). Dwelling for Victor Metzger. Perspective view and ground plan.

PLATE x(a). Hillside Home School building.

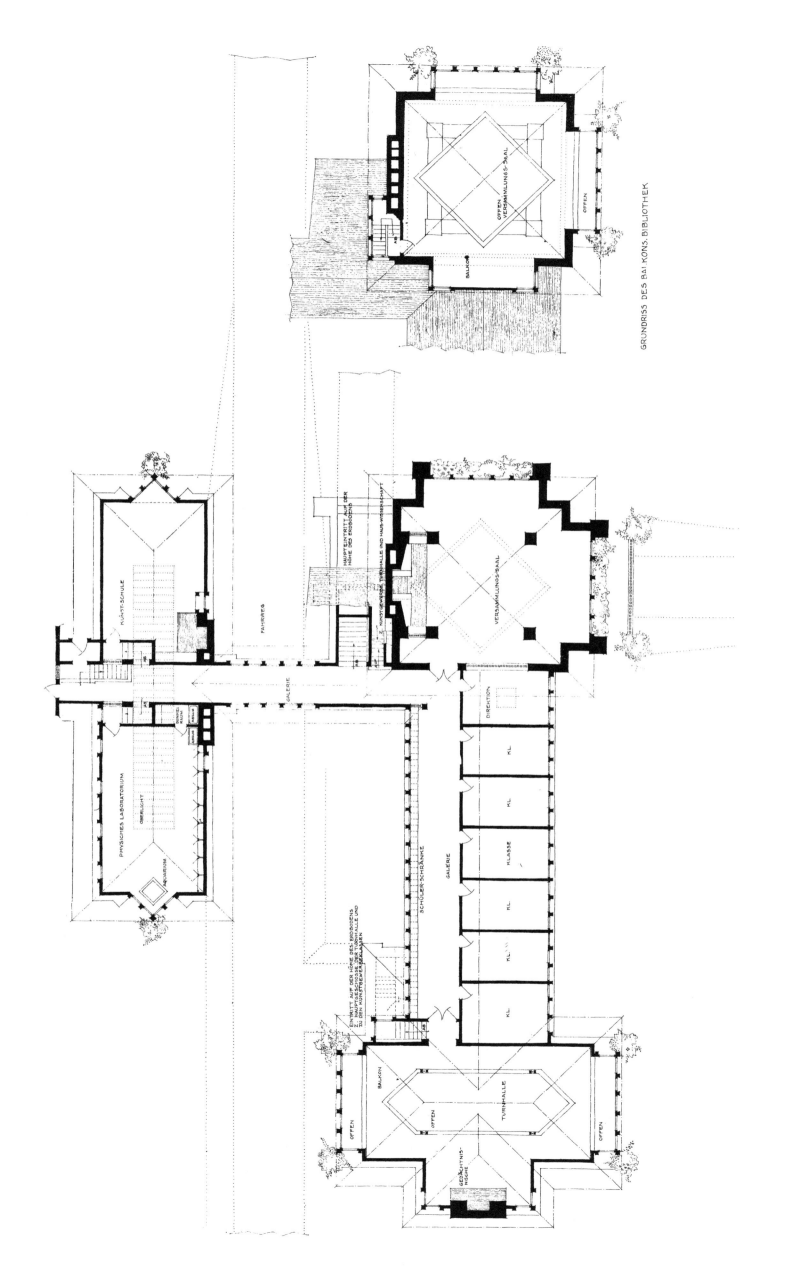

GRUNDRISS DES BAI KONS, BIBLIOTHEK

VERSAMMLUNGS-SAAL

OFFEN

OFFEN

BALKON

KUNST-SCHULE

FAHRWEG

HAUPTEINTRITT AUF DER HÖHE DER ERDBODENS

PHYSISCHES LABORATORIUM

OBERLICHT

AQUARIUM

GALERIE

DUNKEL RAUM

Z. TURNGEWÖLBE, TURNHALLE UND HAUS-WISSENSCHAFT

VERSAMMLUNGS-SAAL

DIREKTION

KL

KL

SCHÜLER-SCHRÄNKE

KLASSE

GALERIE

KL

EINTRITT AUF DER HÖHE DES ERDBODENS
HAUPTEINTRITT Z. HÖHE DER TURNHALLE UND
ZU DEN KUNSTGEWERBE-KLASSEN

KL

KL

OFFEN

BALKON

OFFEN

TURNHALLE

GEDÄCHTNIS-NISCHE

OFFEN

PLATE x(b). Hillside Home School building. Ground plan.

GRUNDRISS DES HAUPTGESCHOSSES

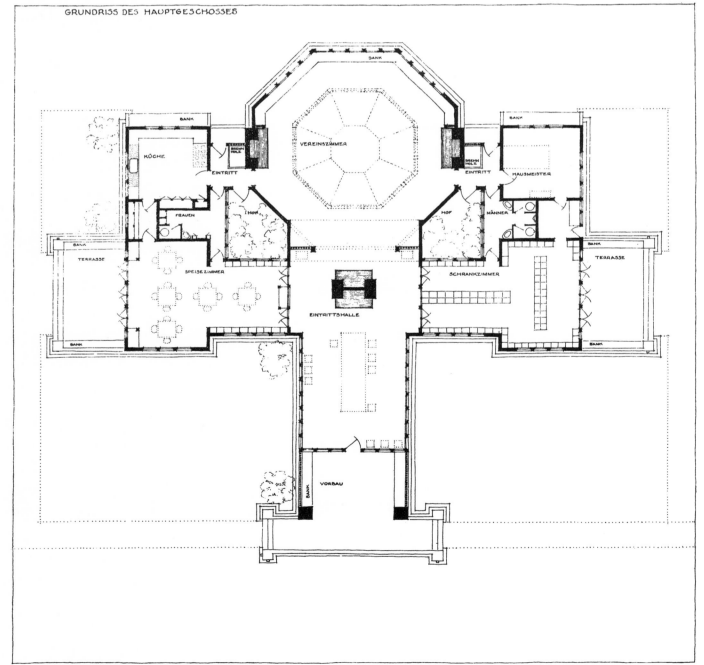

PLATE XI. Forest River Golf Club.

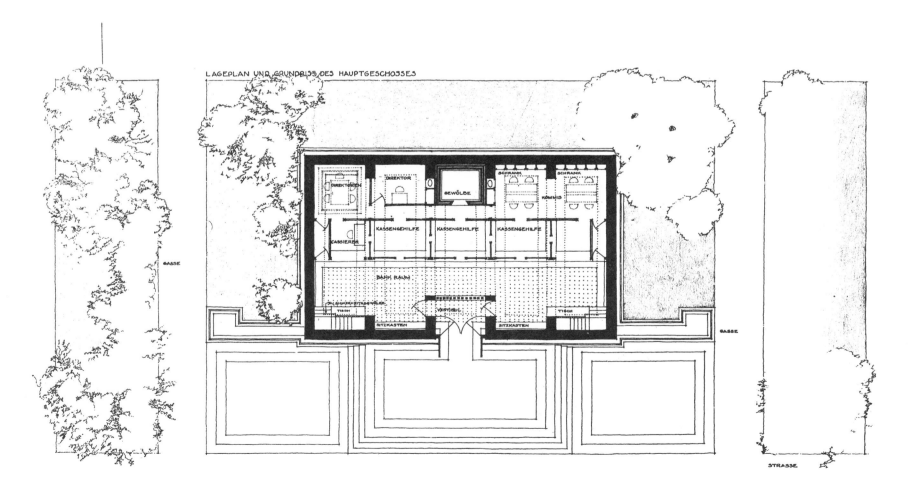

LAGEPLAN UND GRUNDRISS DES HAUPTGESCHOSSES

Plate xii(a). Study for a concrete bank building in a small city.

PLATE XII(b). Study for a concrete bank building in a small city.

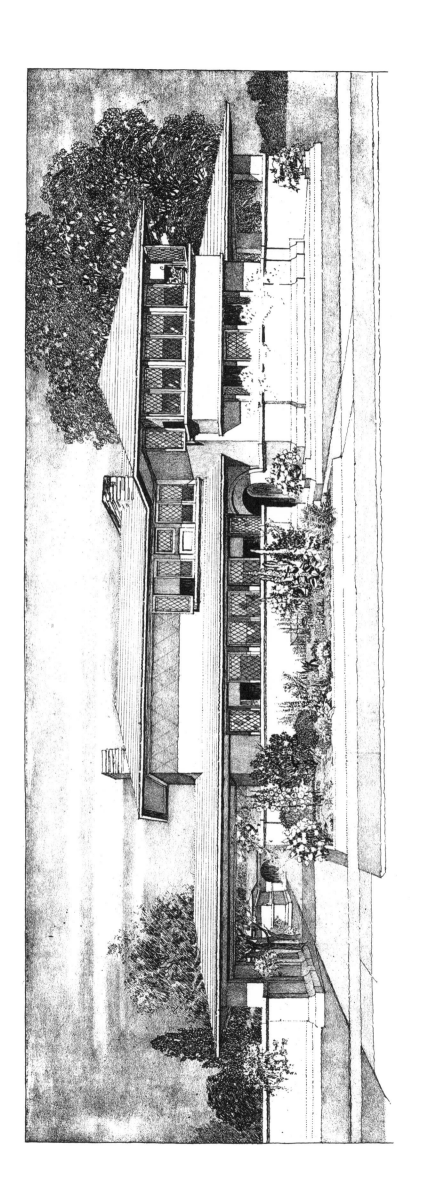

PLATE XIII(a). A typical house intended to form the unit in the group as arranged in the Quadruple Block Plan.

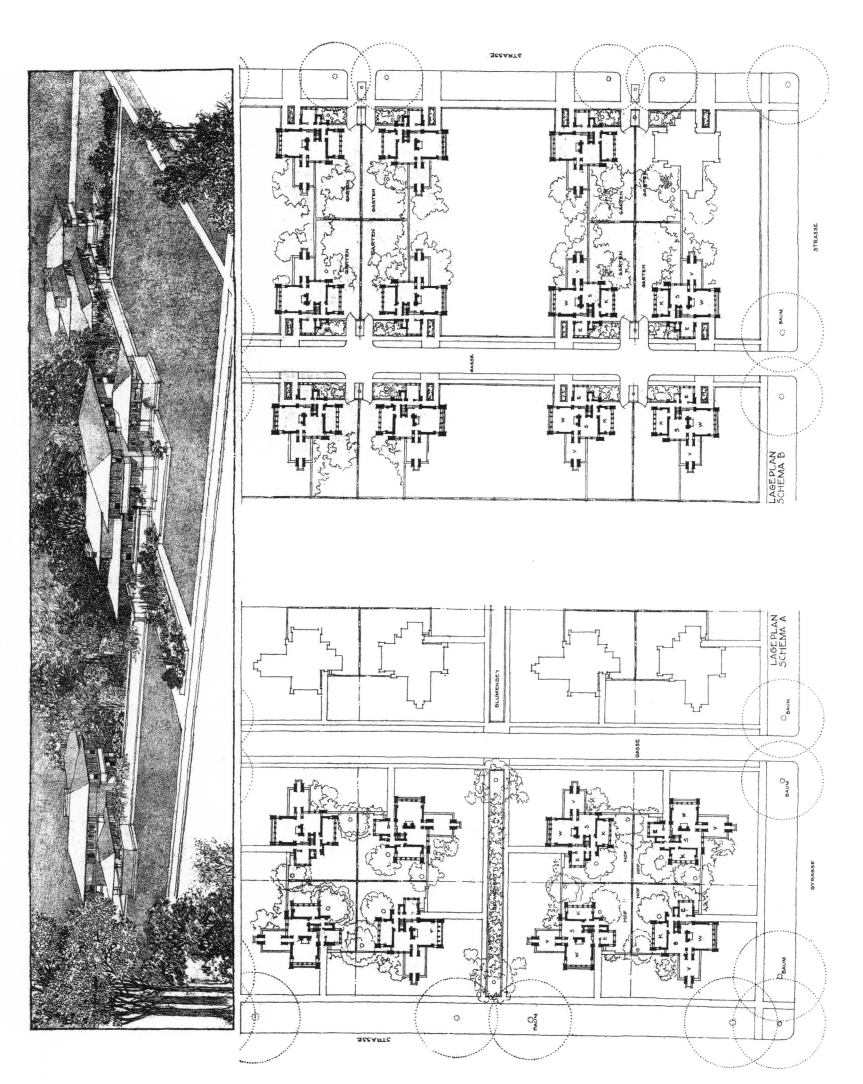

PLATE XIII(b). The Quadruple Block Plan.

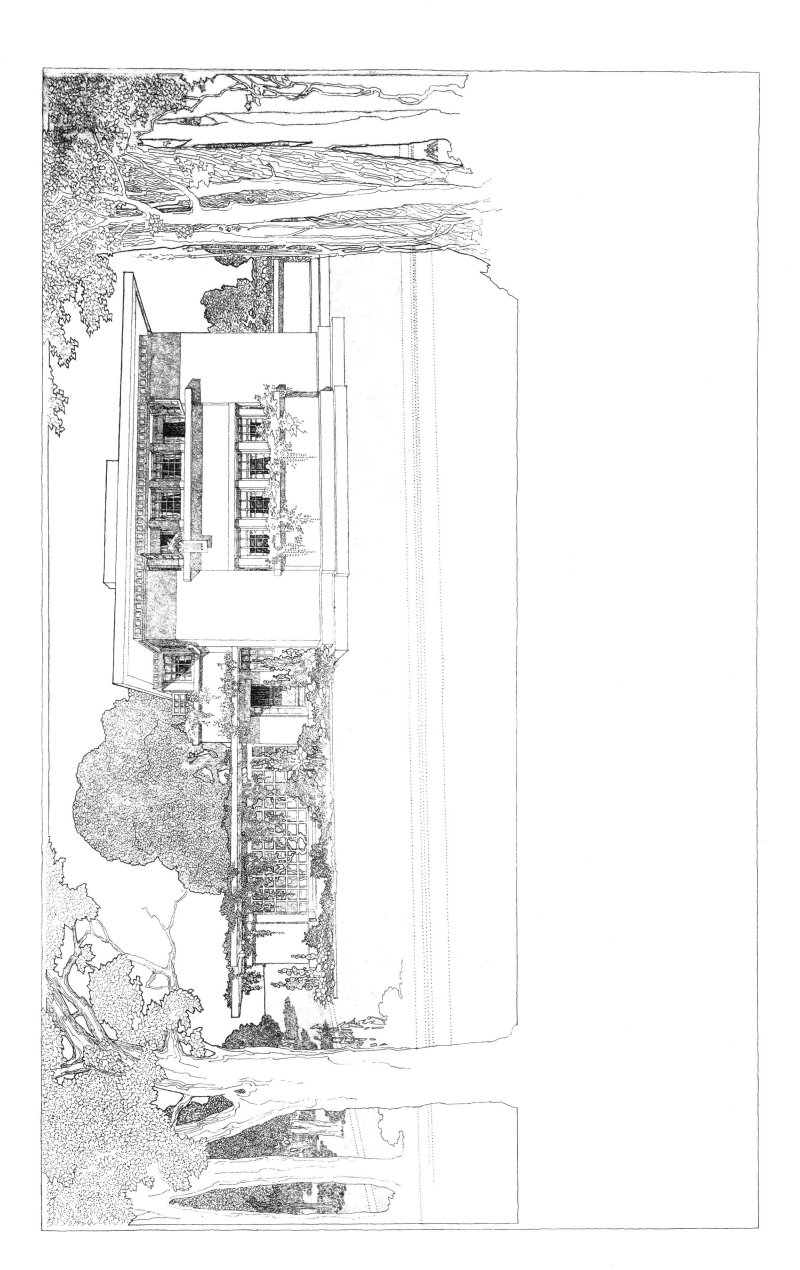

PLATE xiv(a). Concrete house originally designed for *Ladies' Home Journal*. Perspective view.

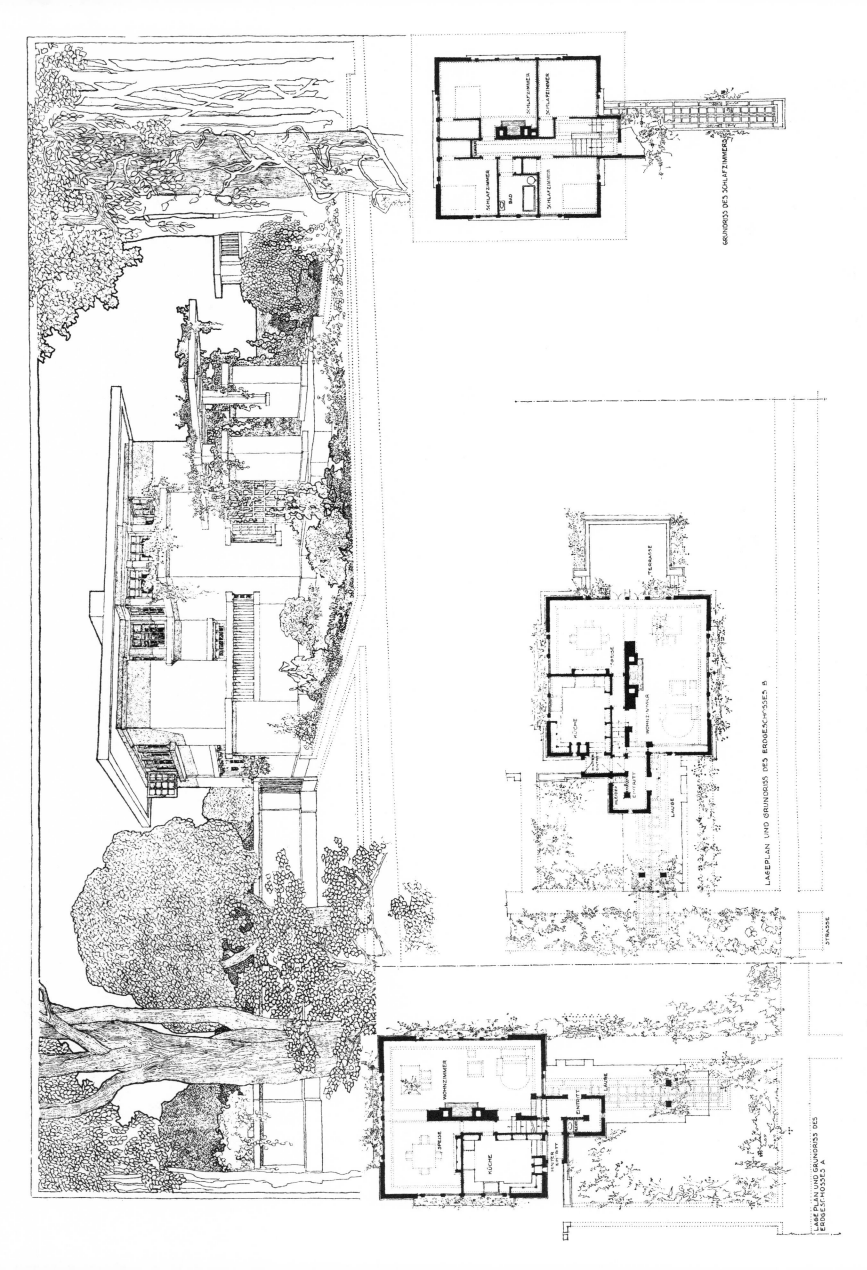

GRUNDRISS DES SCHLAFZIMMERS

SCHLAFZIMMER
SCHLAFZIMMER
SCHLAFZIMMER
BAD
SCHLAFZIMMER

LAGEPLAN UND GRUNDRISS DES ERDGESCHOSSES B

TERRASSE
KÜCHE
SPEISE
WOHNZIMMER
LAUBE
STRASSE

LAGE PLAN UND GRUNDRISS DES ERDGESCHOSSES A

WOHNZIMMER
SPEISE
KÜCHE
HINTER EINTRITT
LAUBE

PLATE XIV(b). Concrete house originally designed for *Ladies' Home Journal*. Perspective view and ground plans.

PLATE xv(a). Perspective view of Thomas P. Hardy house, Racine, Wisc.

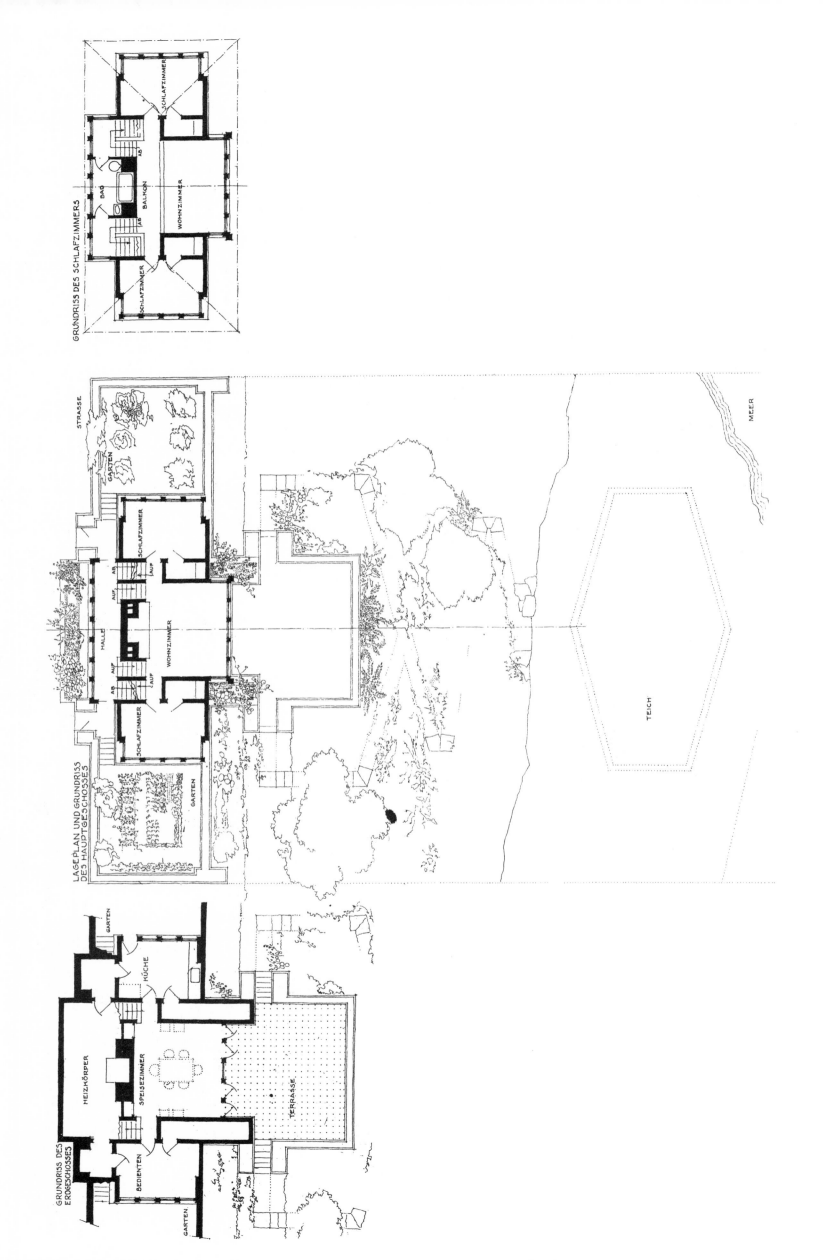

GRUNDRISS DES SCHLAFZIMMERS

SCHLAFZIMMER
SCHLAFZIMMER
BAD
BALKON
AB
AB
WOHNZIMMER

LAGEPLAN UND GRUNDRISS
DES HAUPTGESCHOSSES

STRASSE
GARTEN
SCHLAFZIMMER
AUF
AB
AUF
AB
HALLE
AUF
AUF
WOHNZIMMER
SCHLAFZIMMER
GARTEN
TEICH
MEER

GRUNDRISS DES
ERDGESCHOSSES

GARTEN
KÜCHE
HEIZKÖRPER
SPEISEZIMMER
BEDIENTEN
TERRASSE
GARTEN

PLATE XV(b).   Thomas P. Hardy house. Ground plan.

PLATE XV(c). Thomas P. Hardy house. Perspective view.

PLATE XVI(a). Perspective view of the Ullman house and perspective study for the Westcott house.

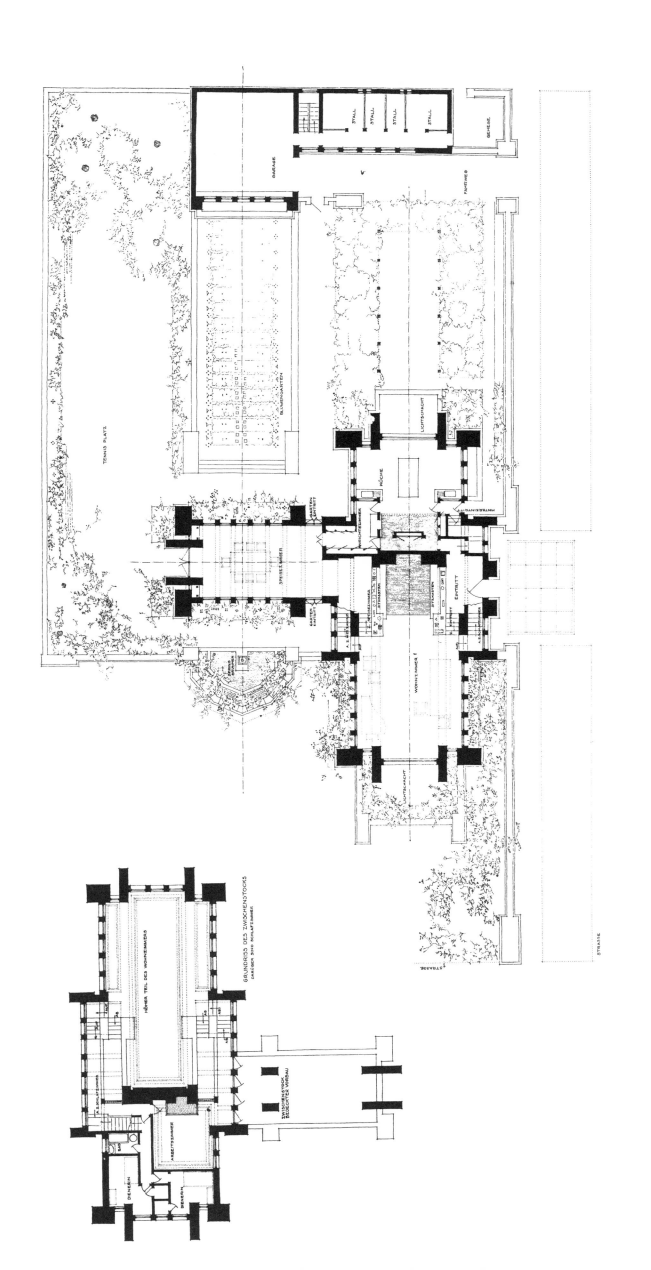

PLATE XVI(b). The Ullman house. Ground plan.

PLATE XVIII(a). Perspective view of dwelling for W. R. Heath, Buffalo, N.Y.

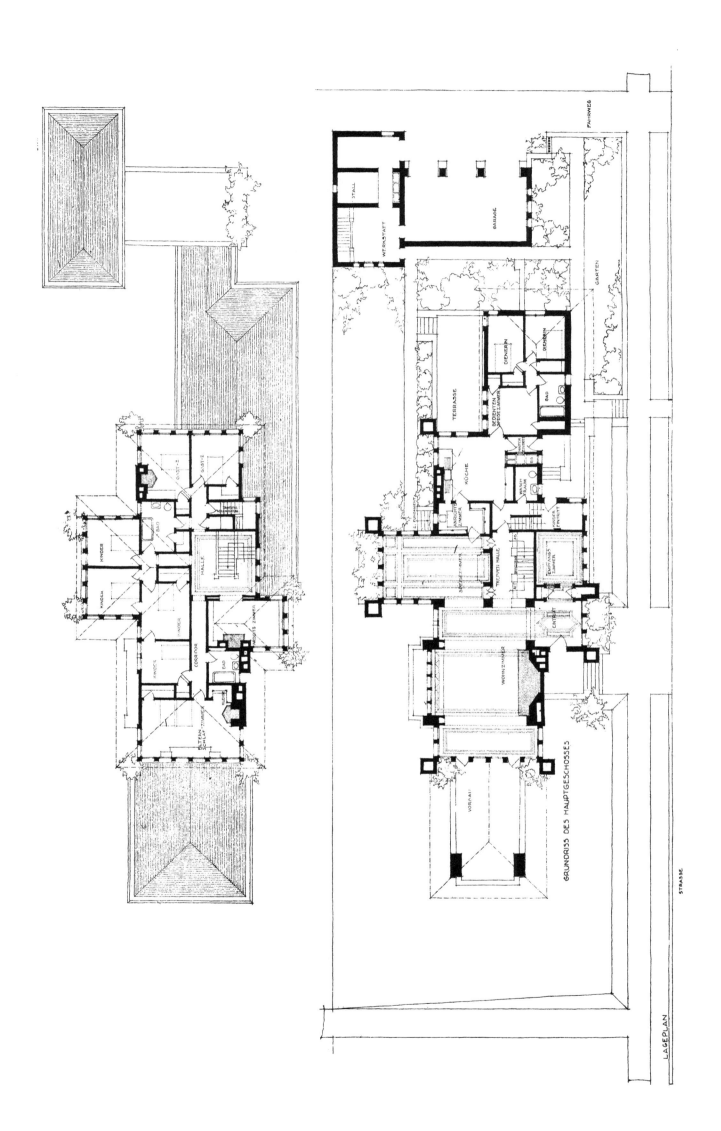

PLATE XVII(b). W. R. Heath house. Ground plan.

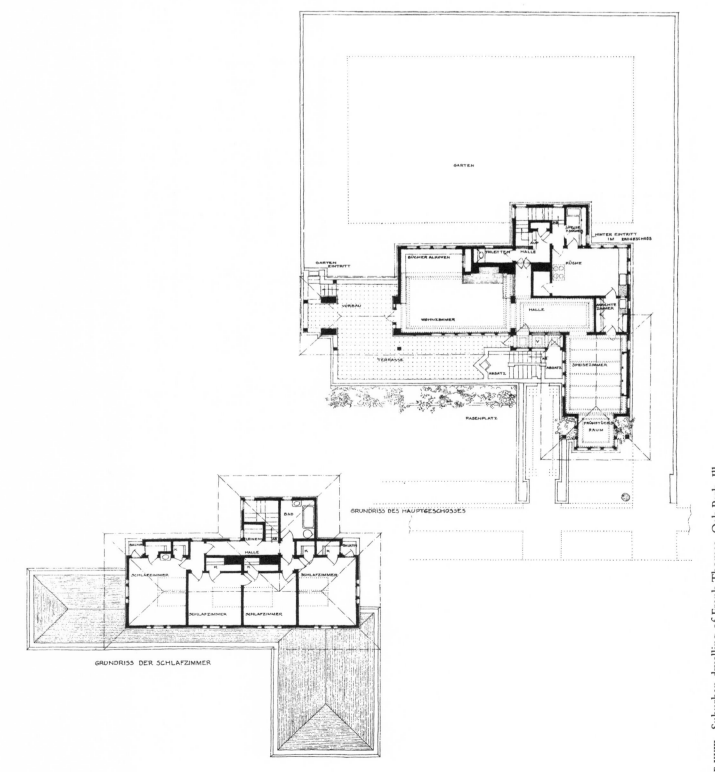

GRUNDRISS DES HAUPTGESCHOSSES

GRUNDRISS DER SCHLAFZIMMER

PLATE XVIII. Suburban dwelling of Frank Thomas, Oak Park, Ill.

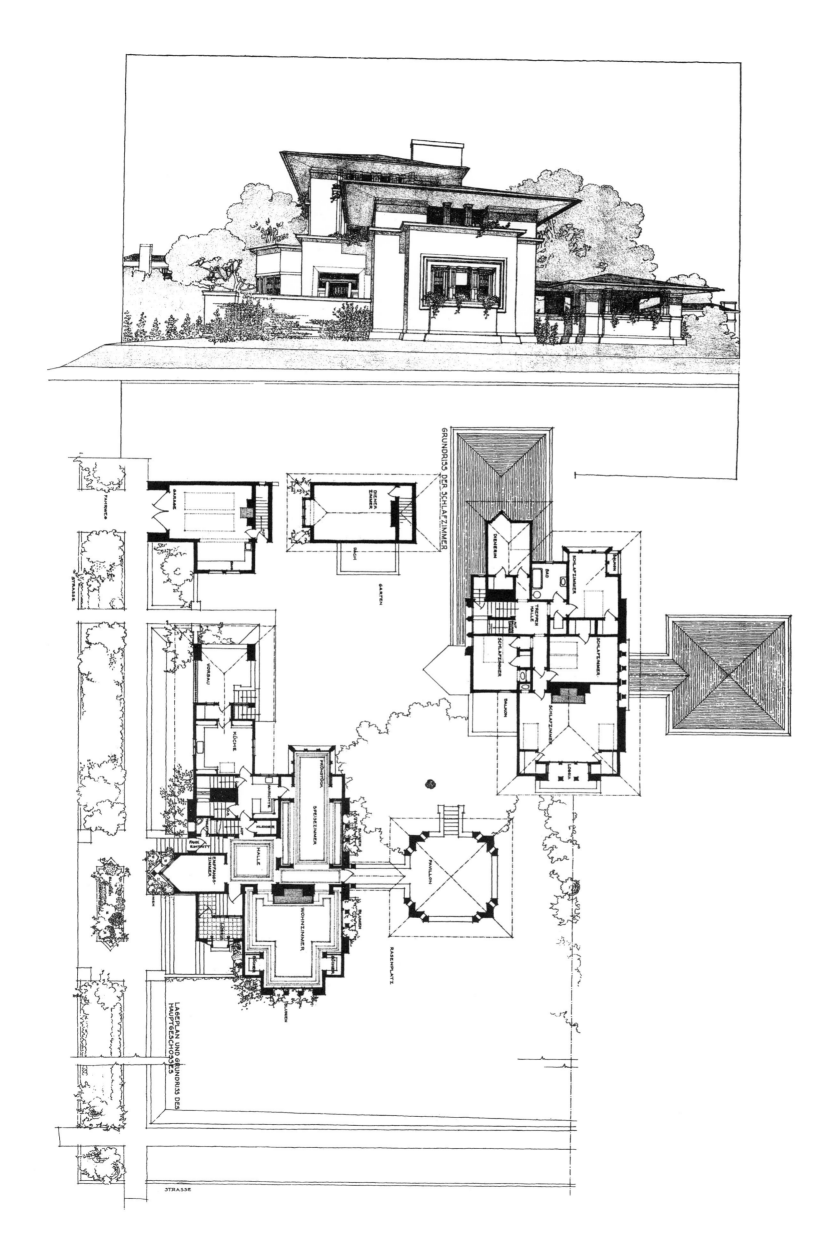

PLATE XIX. Suburban dwelling for Mrs. Martin, Oak Park, Ill.

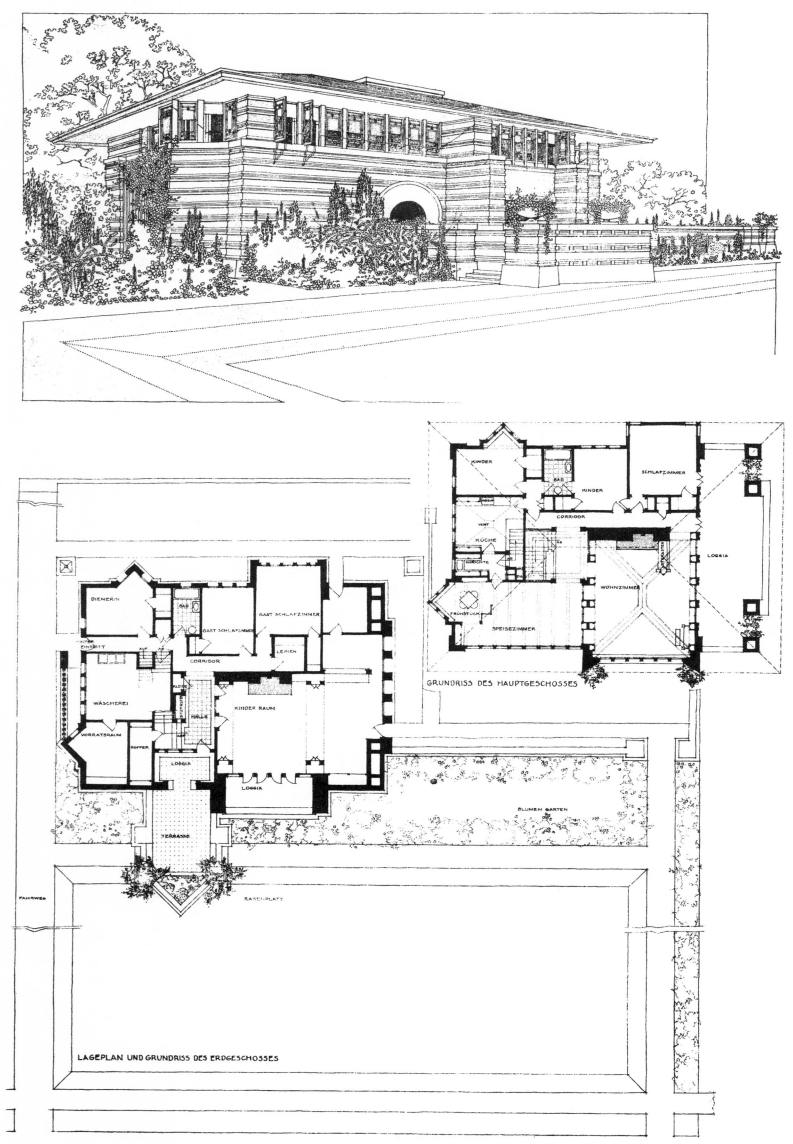

GRUNDRISS DES HAUPTGESCHOSSES

LAGEPLAN UND GRUNDRISS DES ERDGESCHOSSES

PLATE XX. Dwelling of Arthur Heurtley.

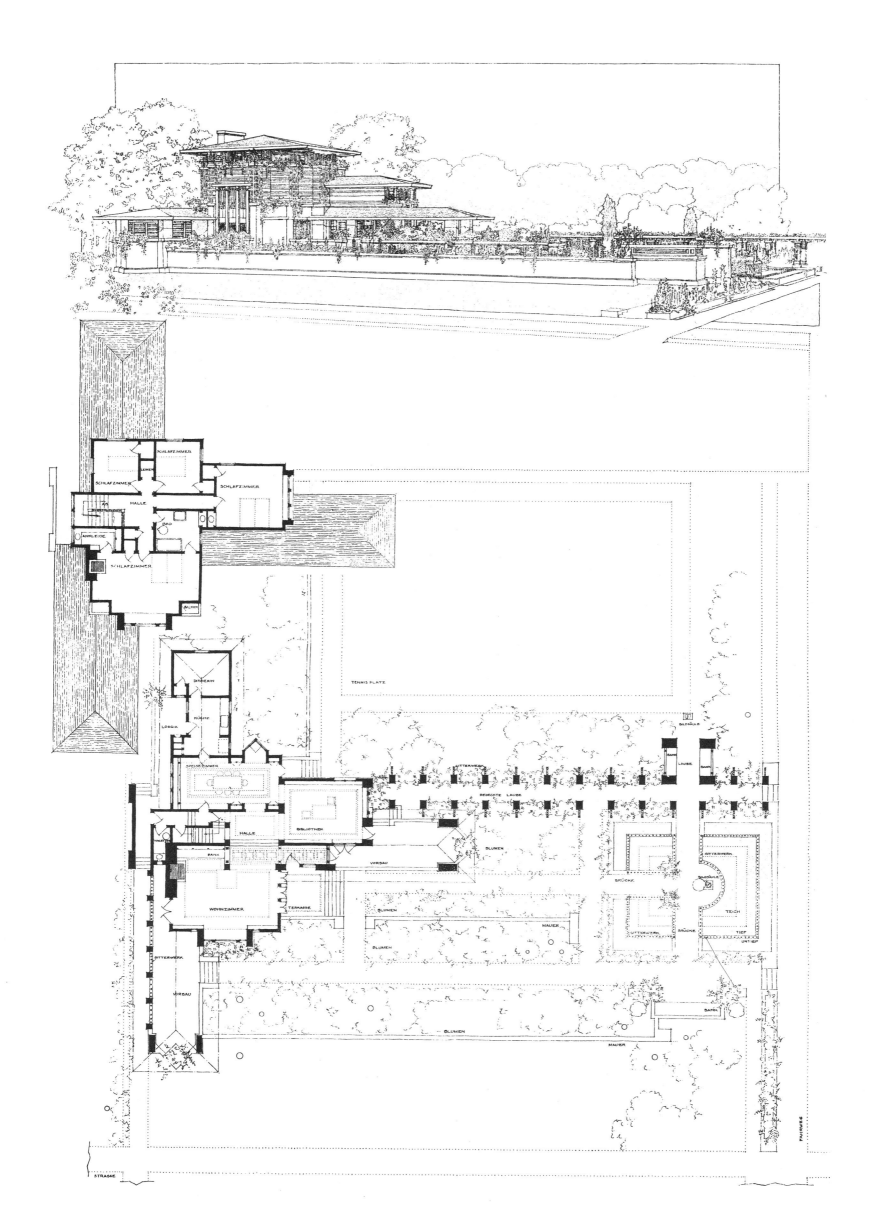

PLATE XXI. Dwelling and garden for W. E. Martin, Oak Park, Ill.

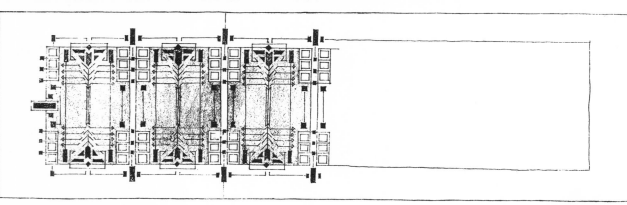

PLATE XXII. Living room in the residence of Harley Bradley, Kankakee, Ill.

PLATE XXIII. Typical low-cost suburban dwelling contributed to the Curtis Publishing Company.

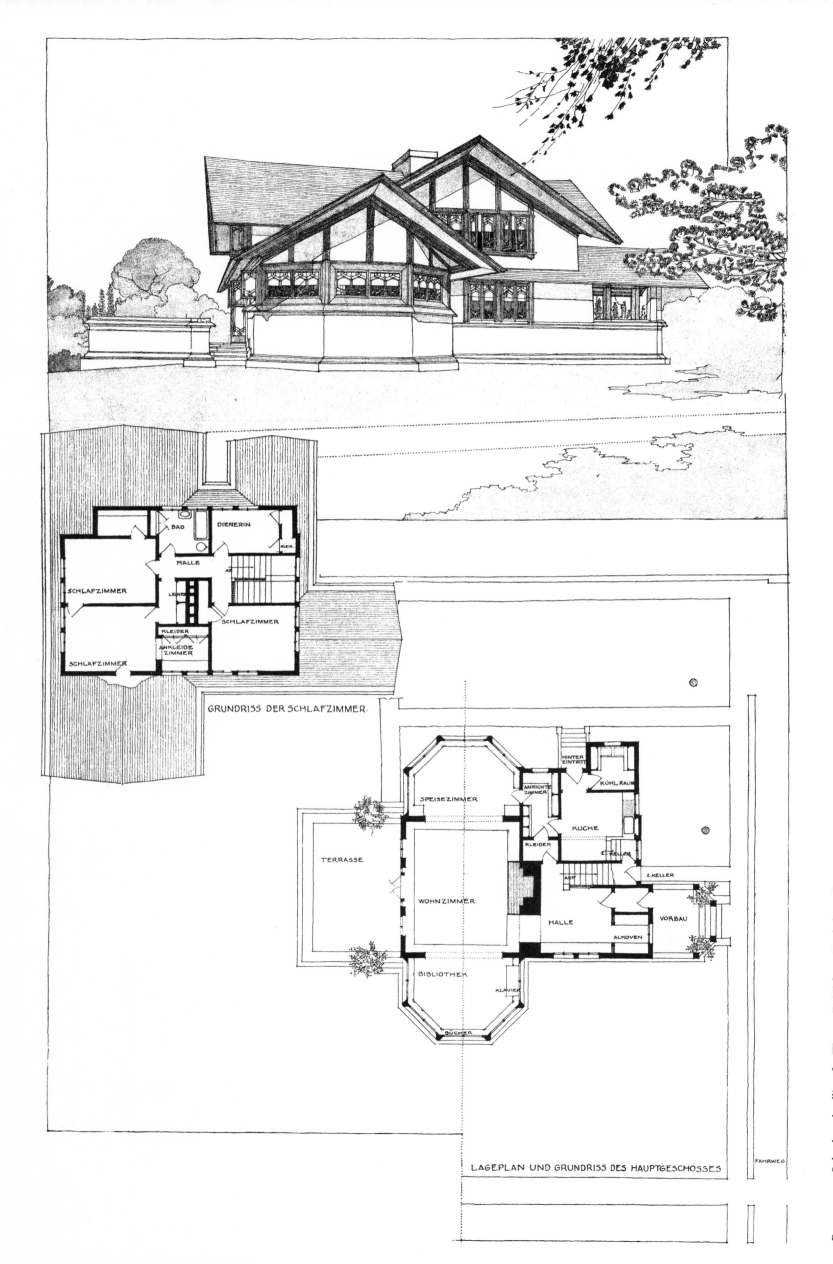

GRUNDRISS DER SCHLAFZIMMER.

DIENERIN
BAD
KLEID.
HALLE
AB.
SCHLAFZIMMER
LEINEN
SCHLAFZIMMER
KLEIDER
ANKLEIDE ZIMMER
SCHLAFZIMMER

SPEISEZIMMER
HINTER EINTRITT
ANRICHT ZIMMER
KÜHL RAUM
KUCHE
TERRASSE
KLEIDER
Z.KELLER
WOHNZIMMER
AUF.
HALLE
VORBAU
ALKOVEN
BIBLIOTHEK
KLAVIER
BÜCHER

LAGEPLAN UND GRUNDRISS DES HAUPTGESCHOSSES

FAHRWEG

PLATE XXIV. Suburban dwelling for Warren F. Hickox, Kankakee, Ill.

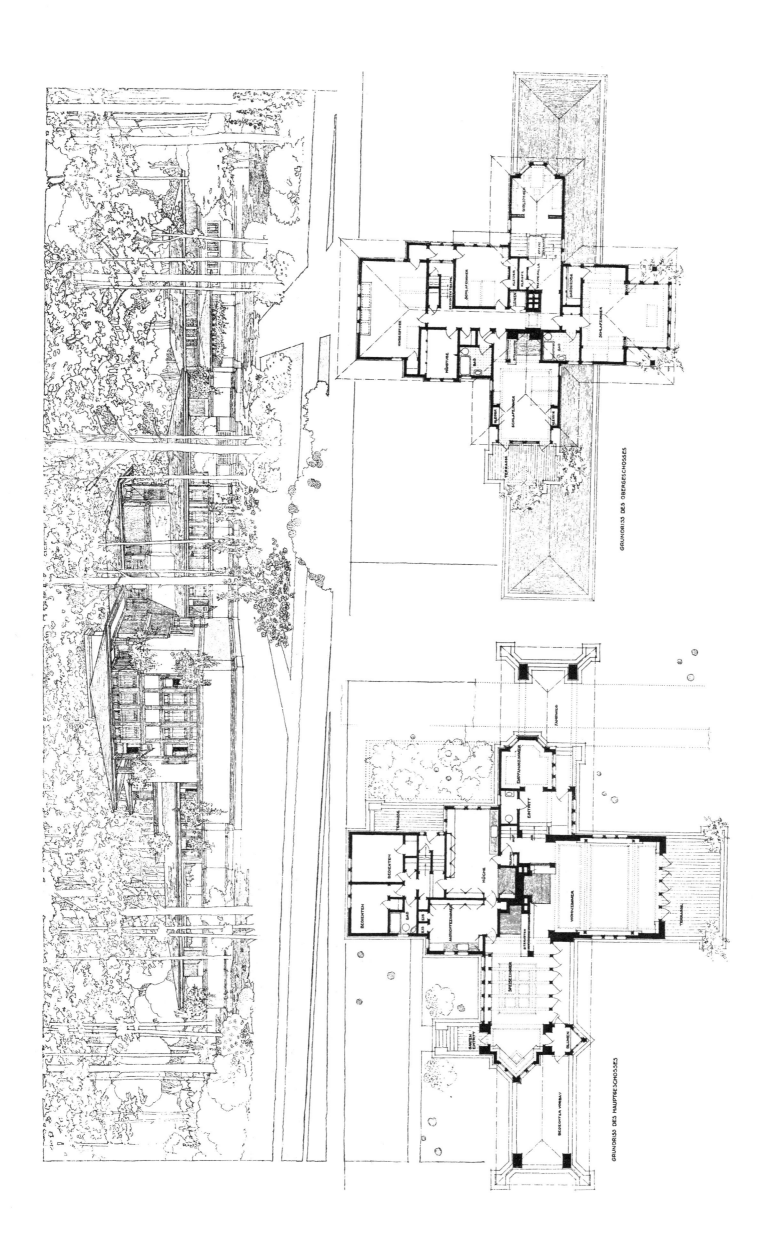

GRUNDRISS DES OBERGESCHOSSES

GRUNDRISS DES HAUPTGESCHOSSES

PLATE XXV. Ground plan and perspective view of Ward W. Willit's villa, Highland Park, Ill.

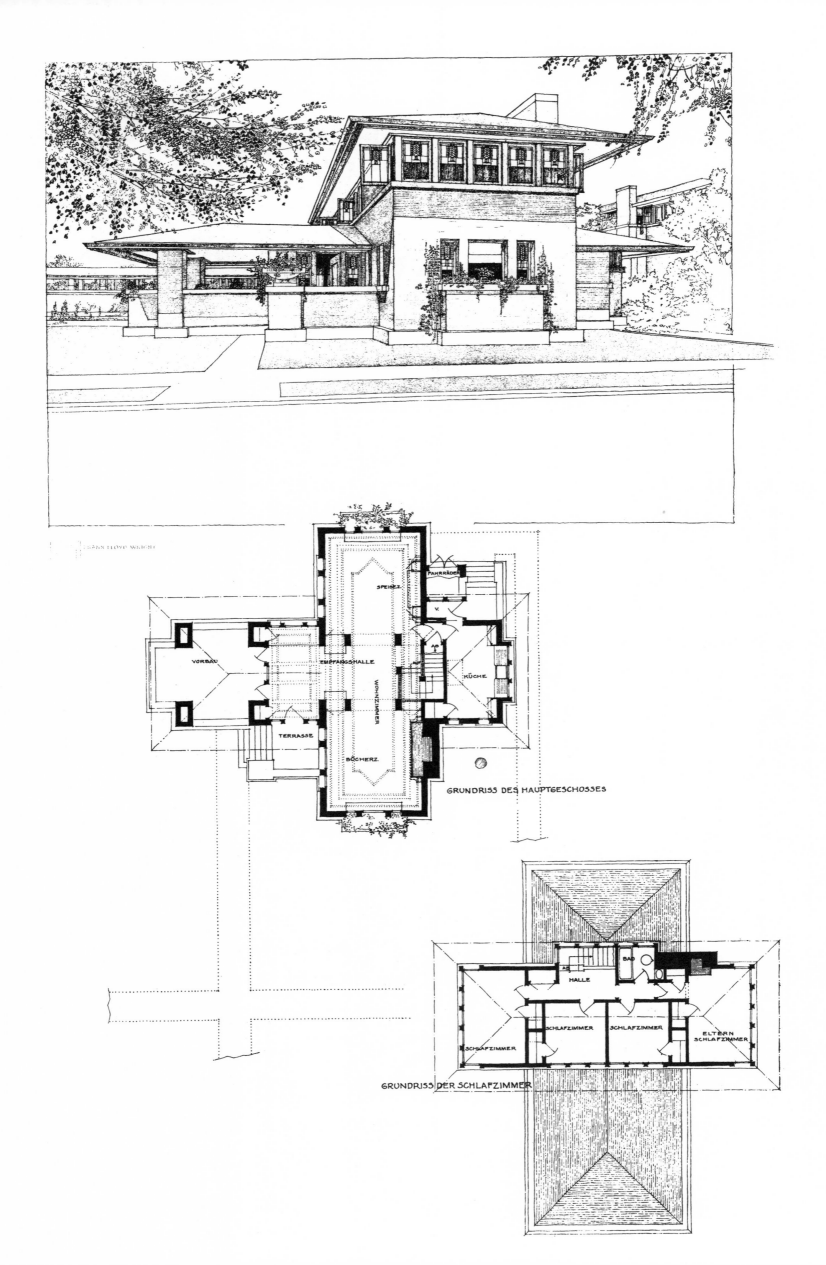

FRANK LLOYD WRIGHT

SPEISEZ.

FAHRRÄDER

V.

VORBAU

EMPFANGSHALLE

KÜCHE

WOHNZIMMER

TERRASSE

BÜCHERZ.

GRUNDRISS DES HAUPTGESCHOSSES

BAD

AB

HALLE

SCHLAFZIMMER

SCHLAFZIMMER

SCHLAFZIMMER

ELTERN
SCHLAFZIMMER

GRUNDRISS DER SCHLAFZIMMER

PLATE XXVI. Masonry dwelling for Mr. Martin, Buffalo, N. Y. Adjoining the Martin residence.

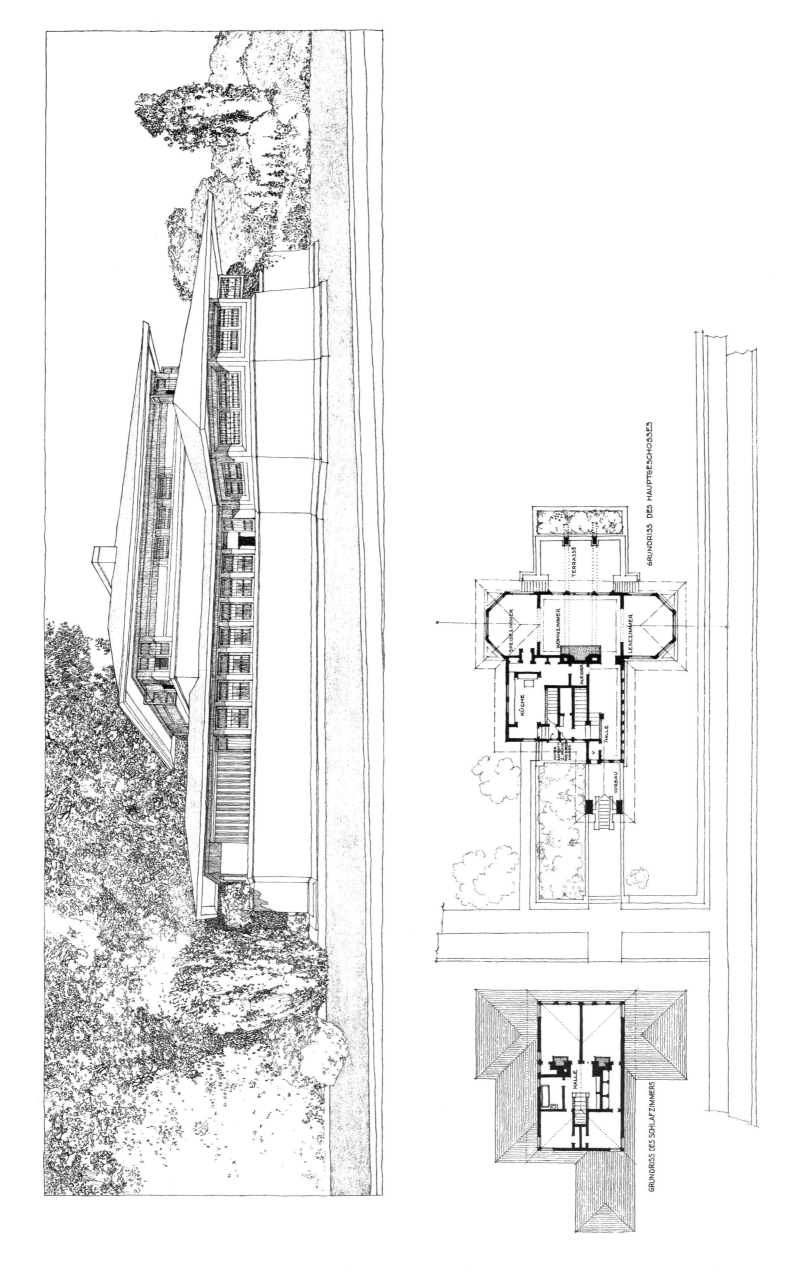

GRUNDRISS DES HAUPTGESCHOSSES

GRUNDRISS DES SCHLAFZIMMERS

PLATE XXVII. Suburban house for Mr. Henderson, Elmhurst, Ill.

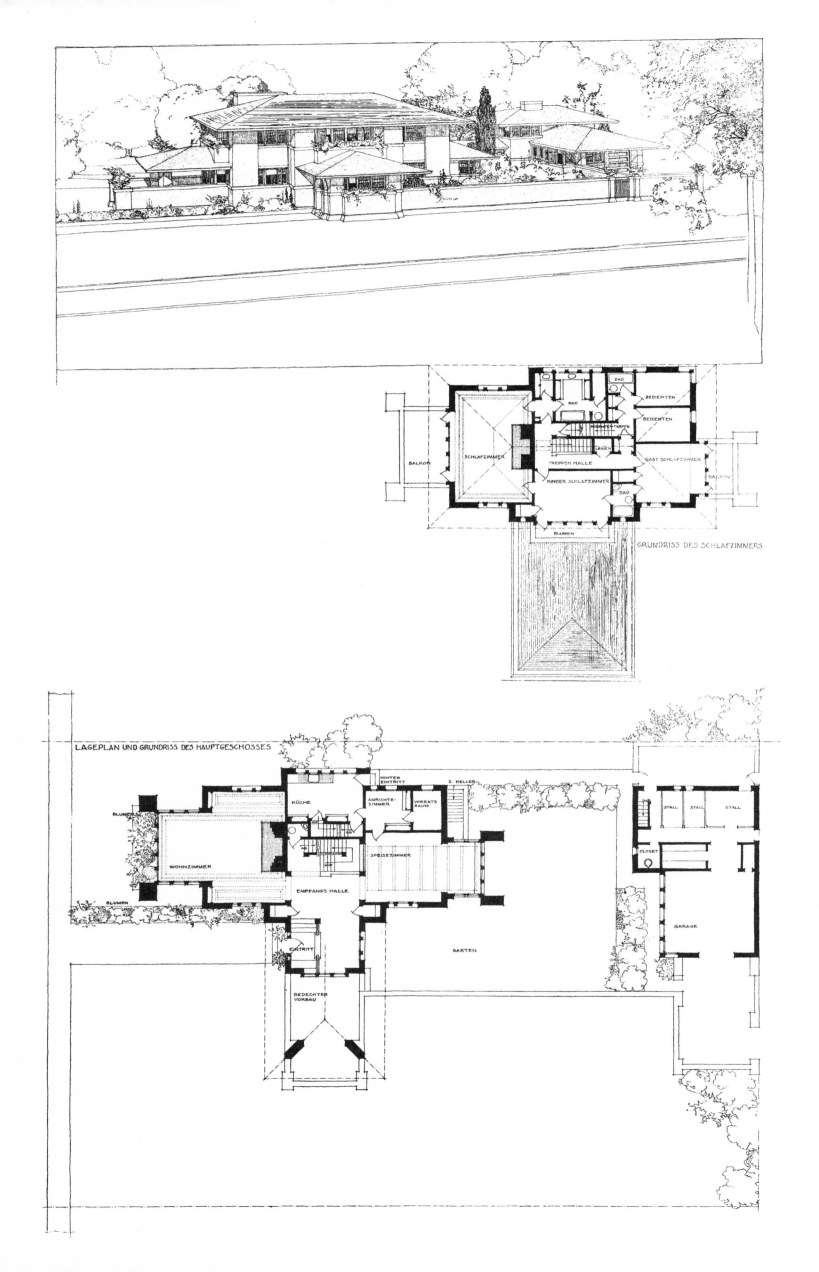

GRUNDRISS DES SCHLAFZIMMERS

BALKON SCHLAFZIMMER TREPPEN HALLE KINDER SCHLAFZIMMER BLUMEN BAD BEDIENTEN BEDIENTEN GAST SCHLAFZIMMER BALKON LEINEN

LAGEPLAN UND GRUNDRISS DES HAUPTGESCHOSSES

BLUMEN WOHNZIMMER KÜCHE ANRICHTE-ZIMMER VORRATS RAUM HINTER EINTRITT Z. KELLER STALL STALL STALL CLOSET SPEISEZIMMER EMPFANGS HALLE BLUMEN EINTRITT BEDECHTER VORBAU GARTEN GARAGE

PLATE XXVII. Residence of F. W. Little, Peoria, Ill.

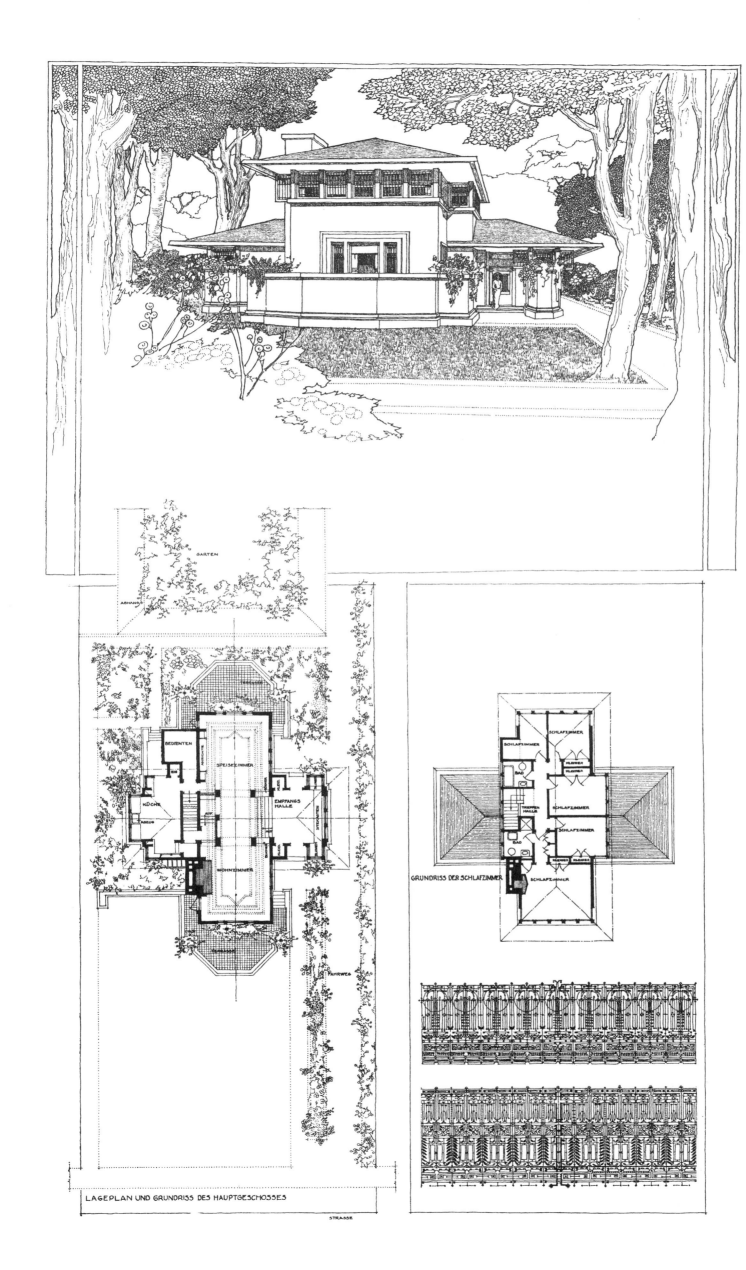

LAGEPLAN UND GRUNDRISS DES HAUPTGESCHOSSES

STRASSE

GRUNDRISS DER SCHLAFZIMMER

PLATE XXIX. House of K. C. De Rhodes at South Bend, Ind.

PLATE XXX(a). Residence of one-story and basement house of E. H. Cheney, Oak Park, Ill.

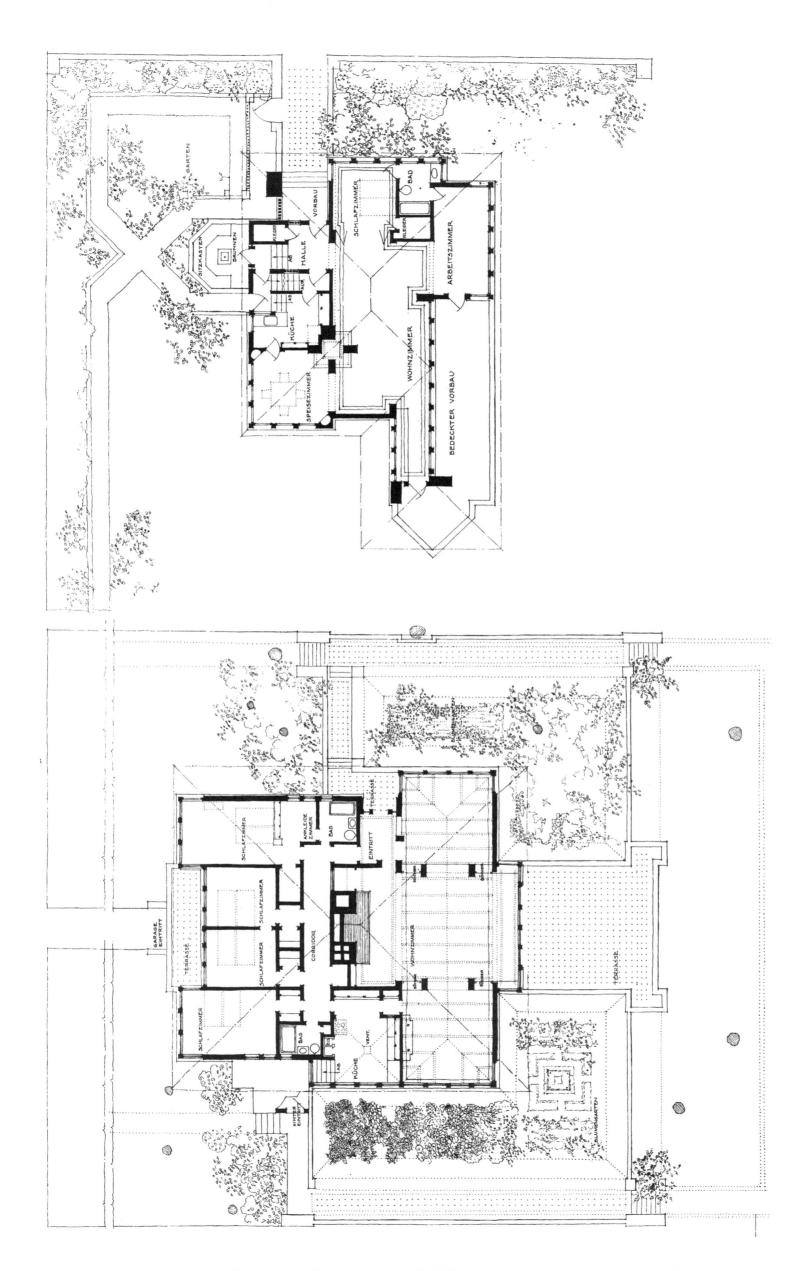

PLATE xxx(b). Ground plan of the E. H. Cheney house and ground plan for a one-story house for an artist.

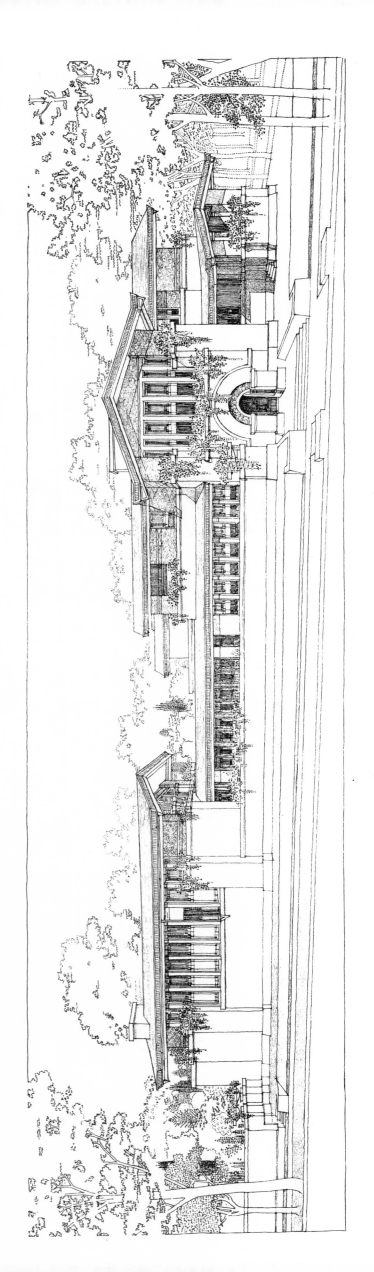

PLATE XXXI(a). General view of a city dwelling for Mrs. Susan L. Dana, Springfield, Ill.

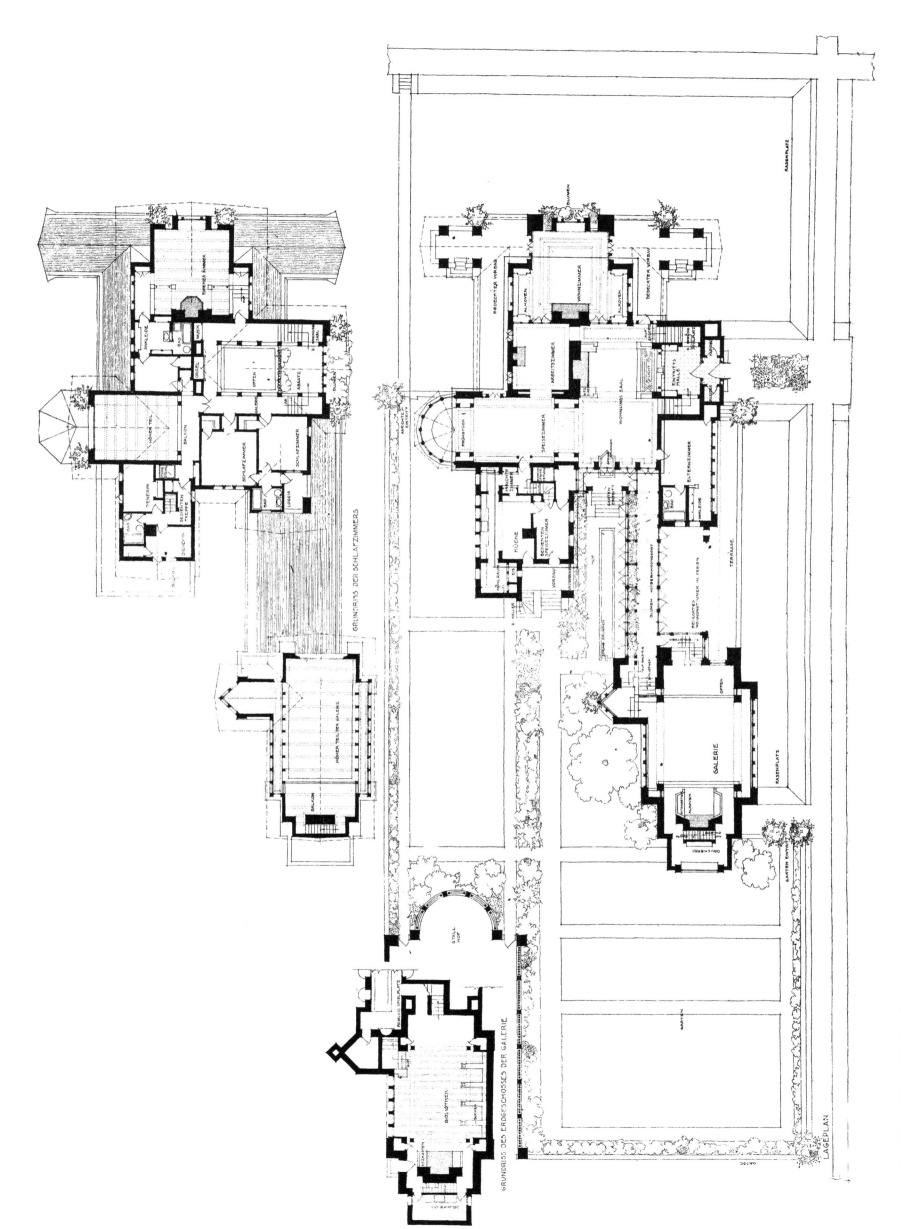

GRUNDRISS DER SCHLAFZIMMERS

GRUNDRISS DES ERDGESCHOSSES DER GALERIE

LAGEPLAN

PLATE XXXI(b). Ground plan of the Dana house.

PLATE XXXI(c). View of the Dana house.

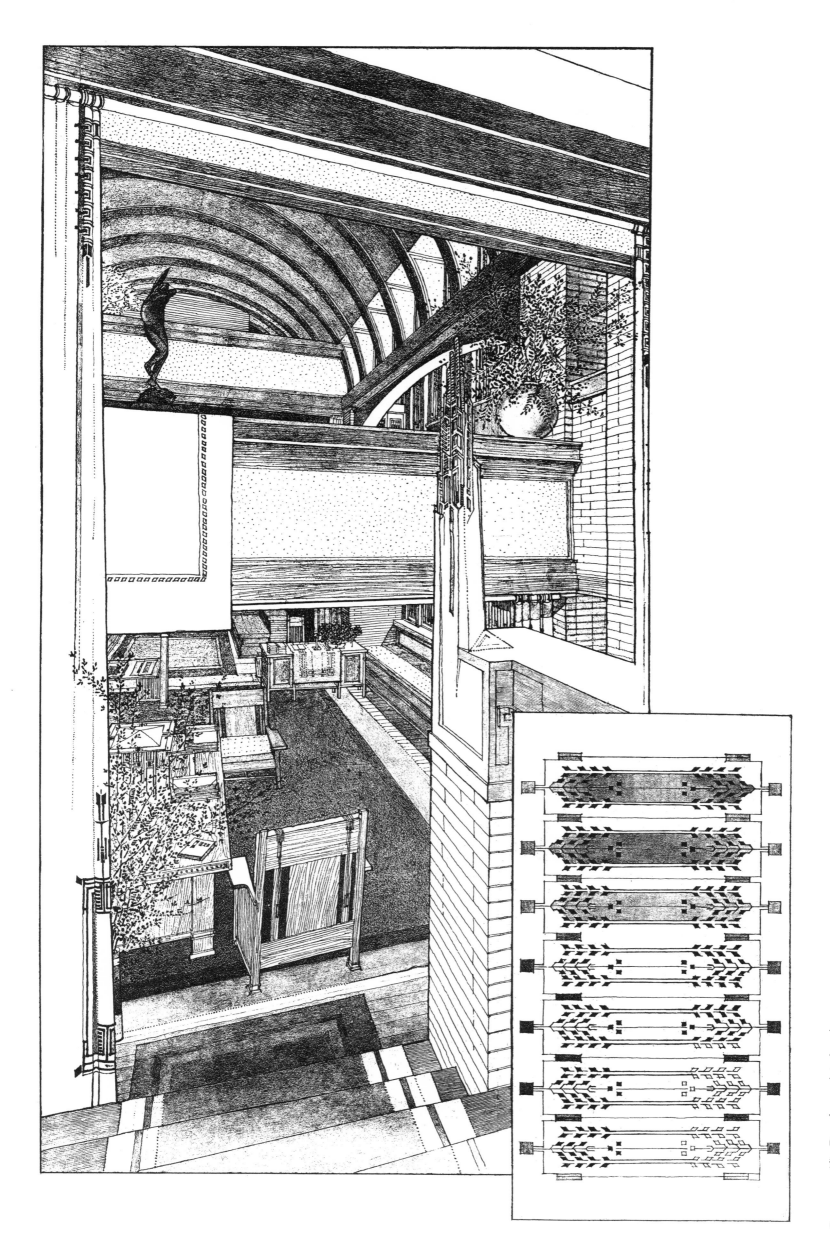

PLATE XXXI(d). Dana house, interior view.

PLATE XXXII(a). Dwelling of D. D. Martin, Buffalo, N. Y.

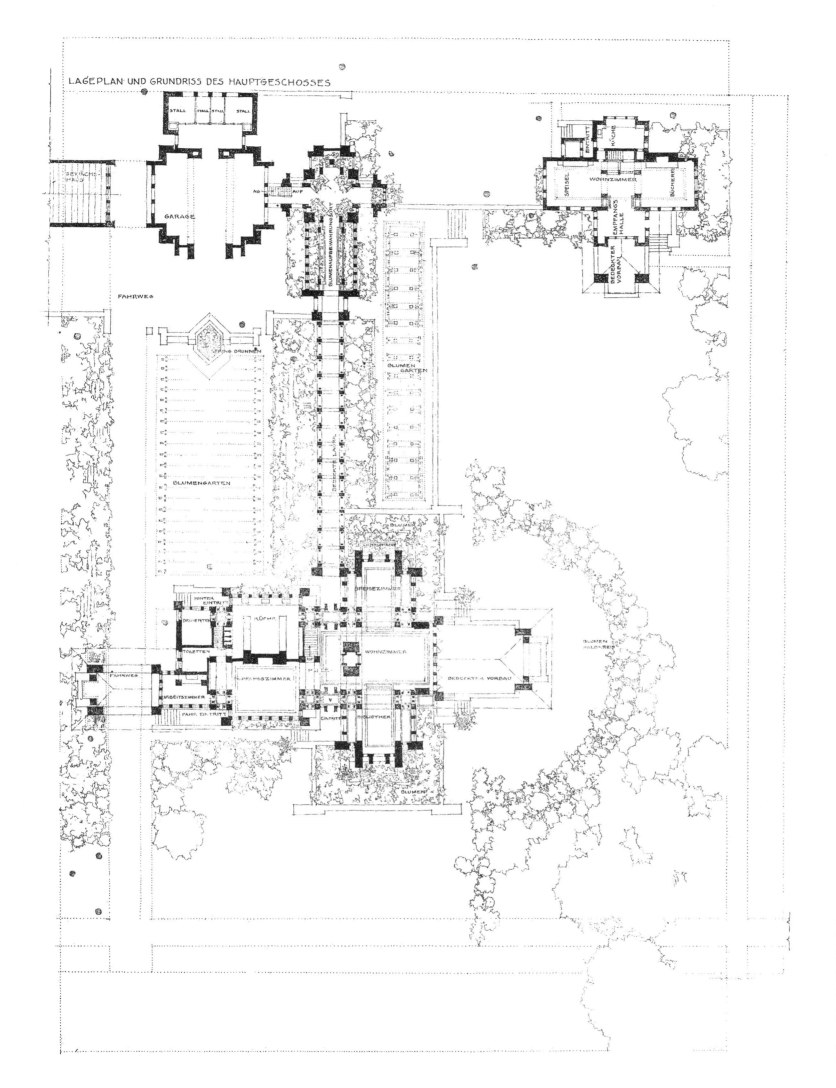

LAGEPLAN UND GRUNDRISS DES HAUPTGESCHOSSES

PLATE XXXII(b). Ground plan of the D. D. Martin house.

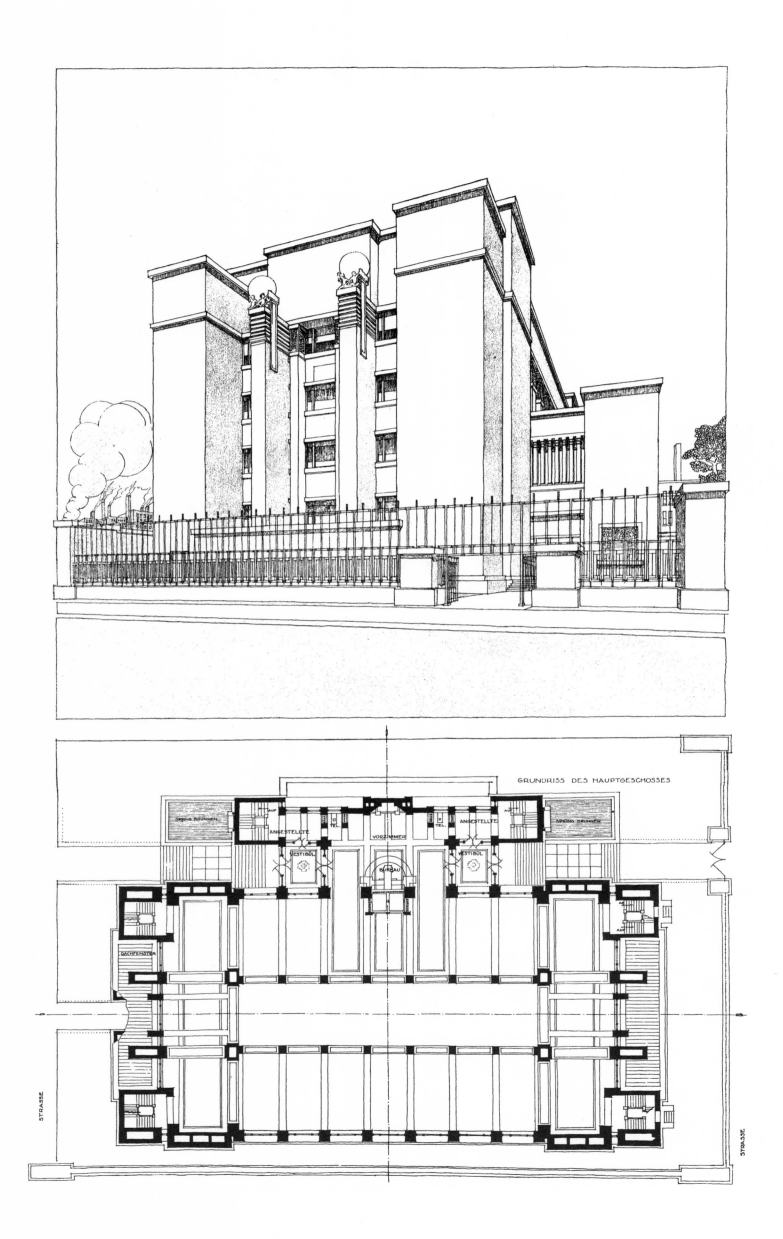

GRUNDRISS DES HAUPTGESCHOSSES

PLATE xxxiii(a). Ground plan and perspective view of the administration building of the Larkin Company.

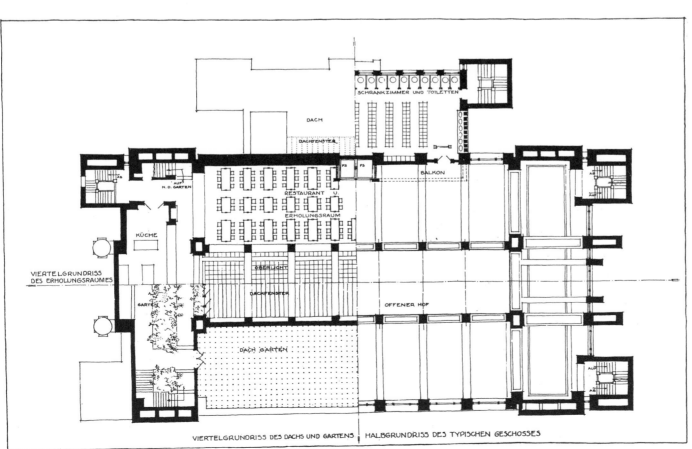

SCHRANKZIMMER UND TOILETTEN

DACH

DACHFENSTER

BALKON

RESTAURANT U. ERHOLUNGSRAUM

AUF N. D. GARTEN

KÜCHE

VIERTELGRUNDRISS DES ERHOLUNGSRAUMES

OBERLICHT

GARTEN

DACHFENSTER

OFFENER HOF

DACH GARTEN

VIERTELGRUNDRISS DES DACHS UND GARTENS | HALBGRUNDRISS DES TYPISCHEN GESCHOSSES

PLATE XXXIII(b). Ground plan and perspective view of the administration building of the Larkin Company.

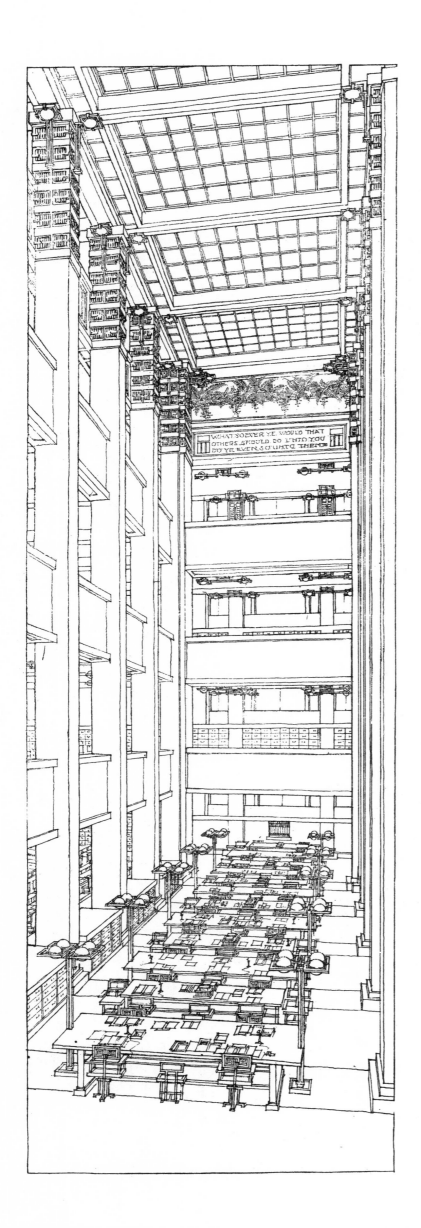

PLATE XXXIII(c). Administration building of the Larkin Company, interior.

PLATE XXXIV(a). Country house for C. Thaxter Shaw, Montreal, Canada.

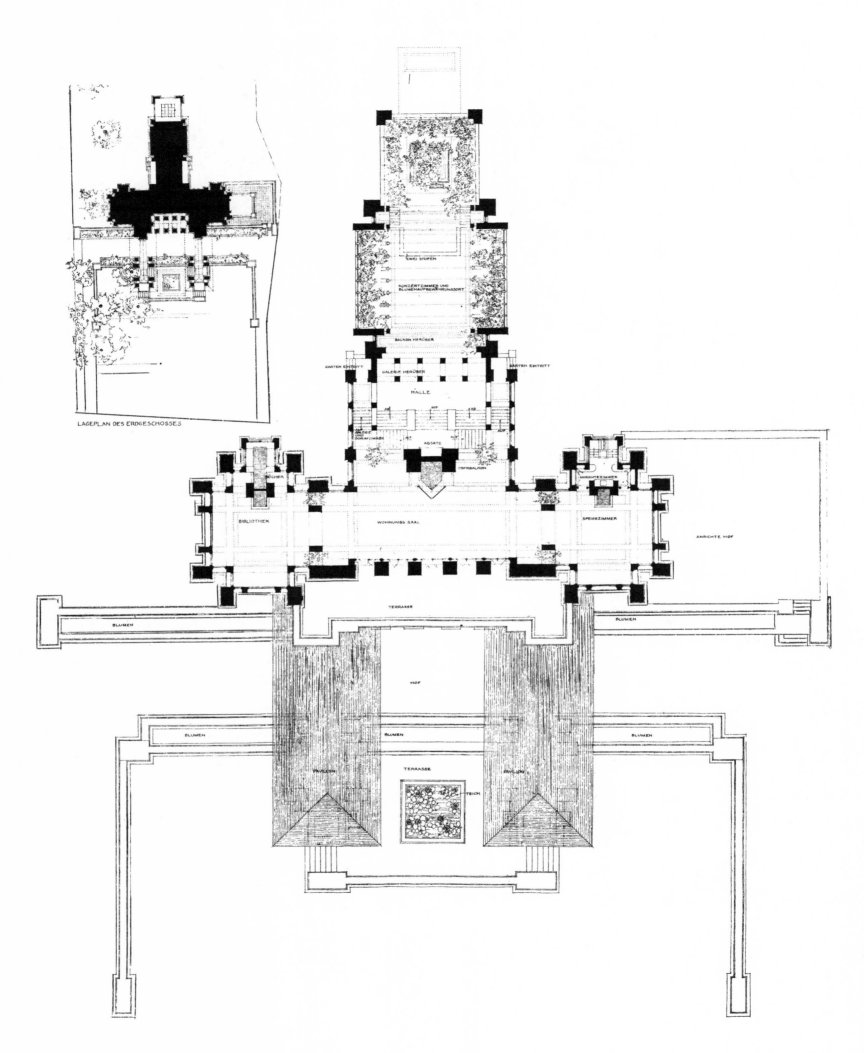

LAGEPLAN DES ERDGESCHOSSES

PLATE XXXIV(b). Ground plan of the C. Thaxter Shaw house.

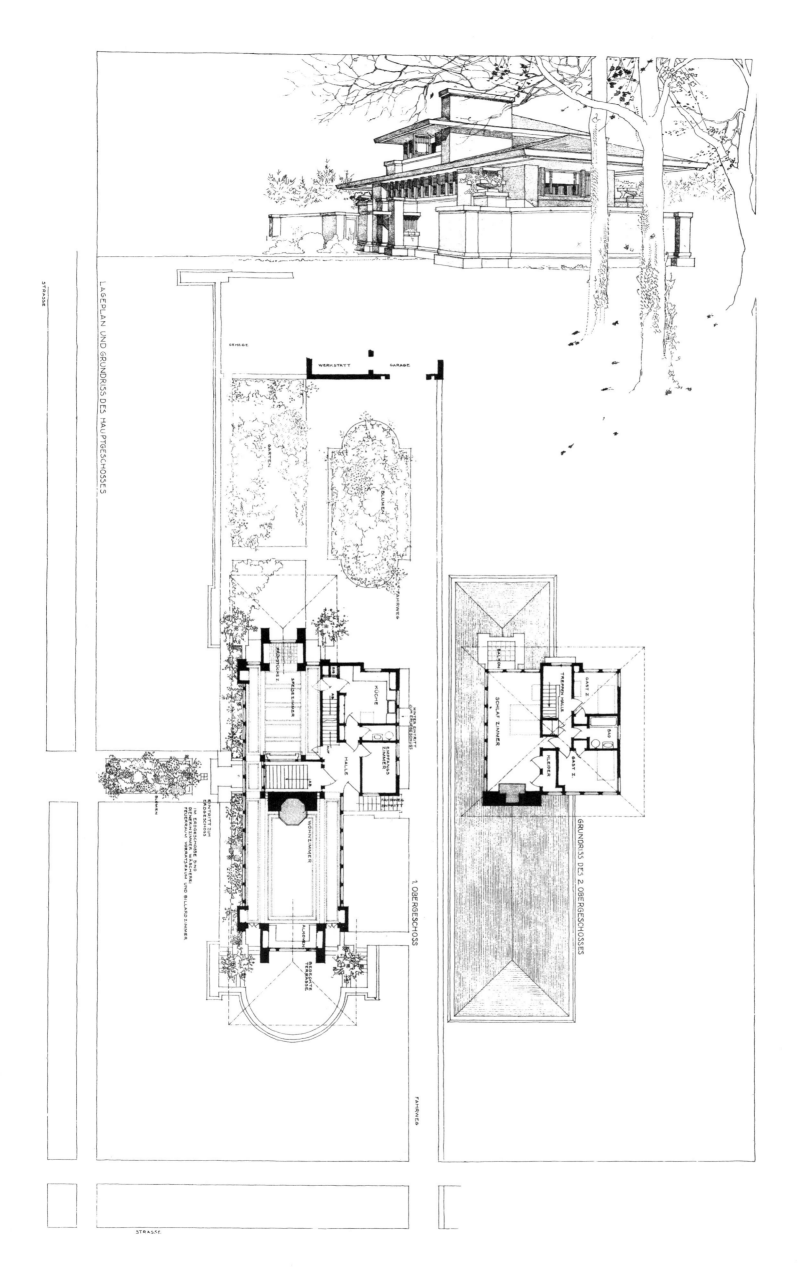

LAGEPLAN UND GRUNDRISS DES HAUPTGESCHOSSES

GEHEGE

WERKSTATT   GARAGE.

GARTEN

BLUMEN

FAHRWEG

1. OBERGESCHOSS

HAUPTSCHLAFZ

SPEISEZIMMER

KÜCHE

HINTER EINTRITT ZUM ERDGESCHOSS

EMPFANGS ZIMMER

HALLE

FAHRWEG

EINTRITT ZUM ERDGESCHOSS
IM ERDGESCHOSS SIND
DIE DIENSTZIMMER, WÄSCHEREI
FEUERRAUM VORRATSRAUM UND BILLARD ZIMMER

WOHNZIMMER

BLUMEN

STRASSE

BLUMEN

AUSSEN
GEDECKTE VERANDA

GRUNDRISS DES 2. OBERGESCHOSSES

BALKON

SCHLAF ZIMMER

TREPPEN HALLE

GAST Z

BAD

KLEIDER

GAST Z.

FAHRWEG

STRASSE

PLATE XXXV. Suburban residence for Mr. Tomek, Riverside, Ill.

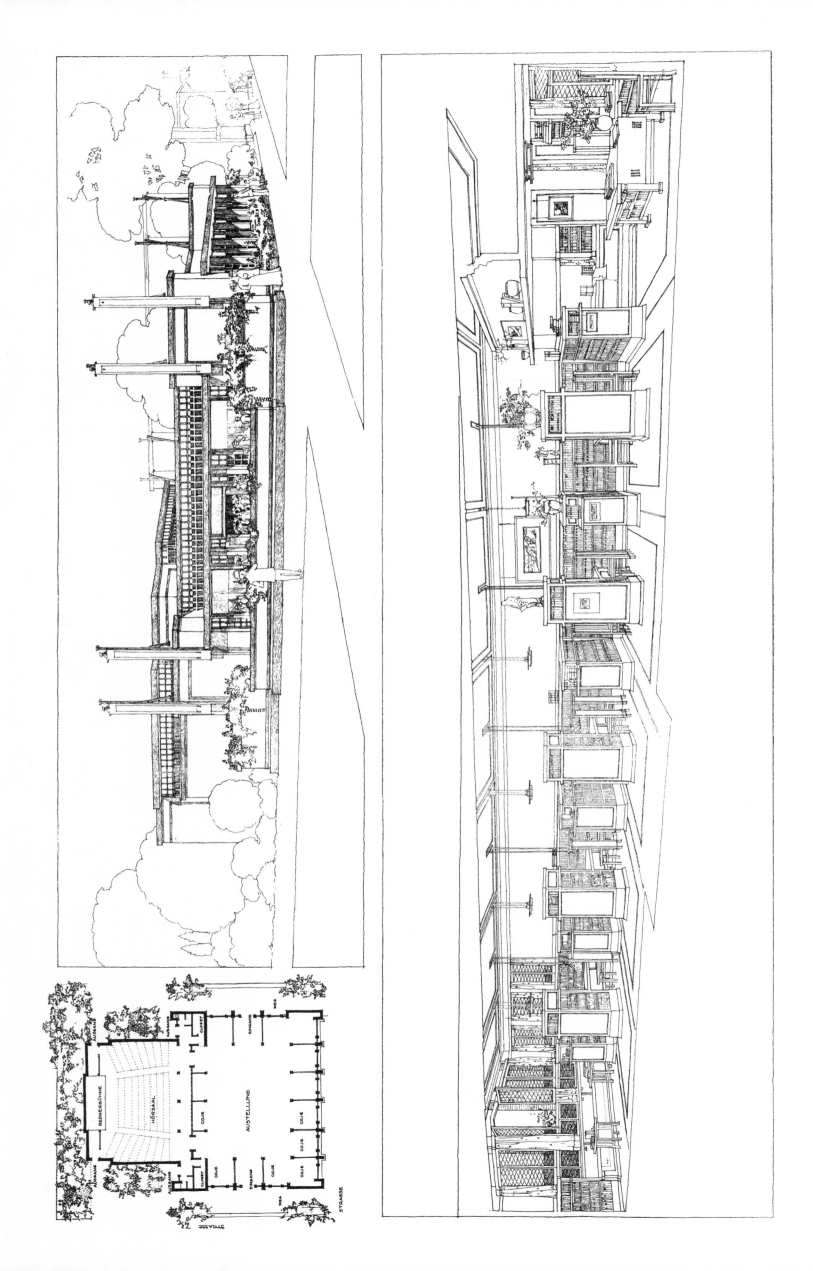

PLATE XXXVI. Exposition building for the Larkin Company. Browne's Bookstore.

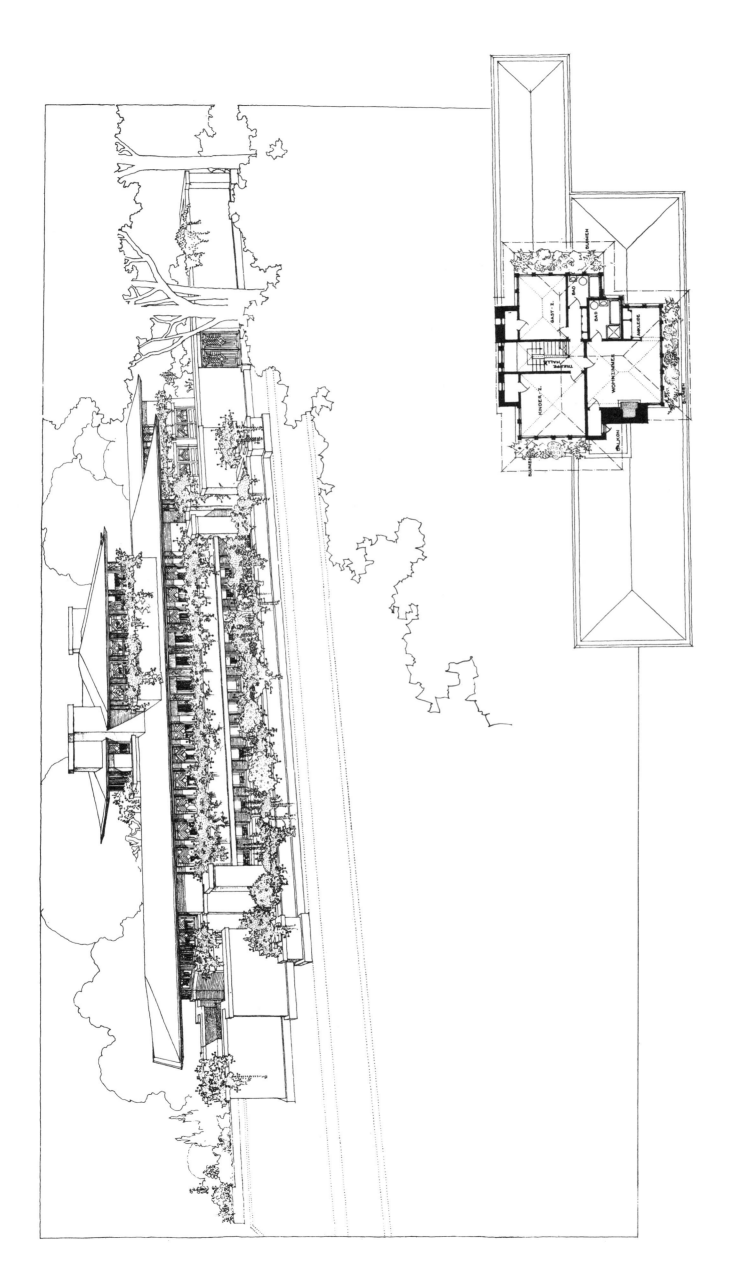

PLATE XXXVII(a). City dwelling of Fred C. Robie, Woodlawn Ave. and 57th St., Chicago.

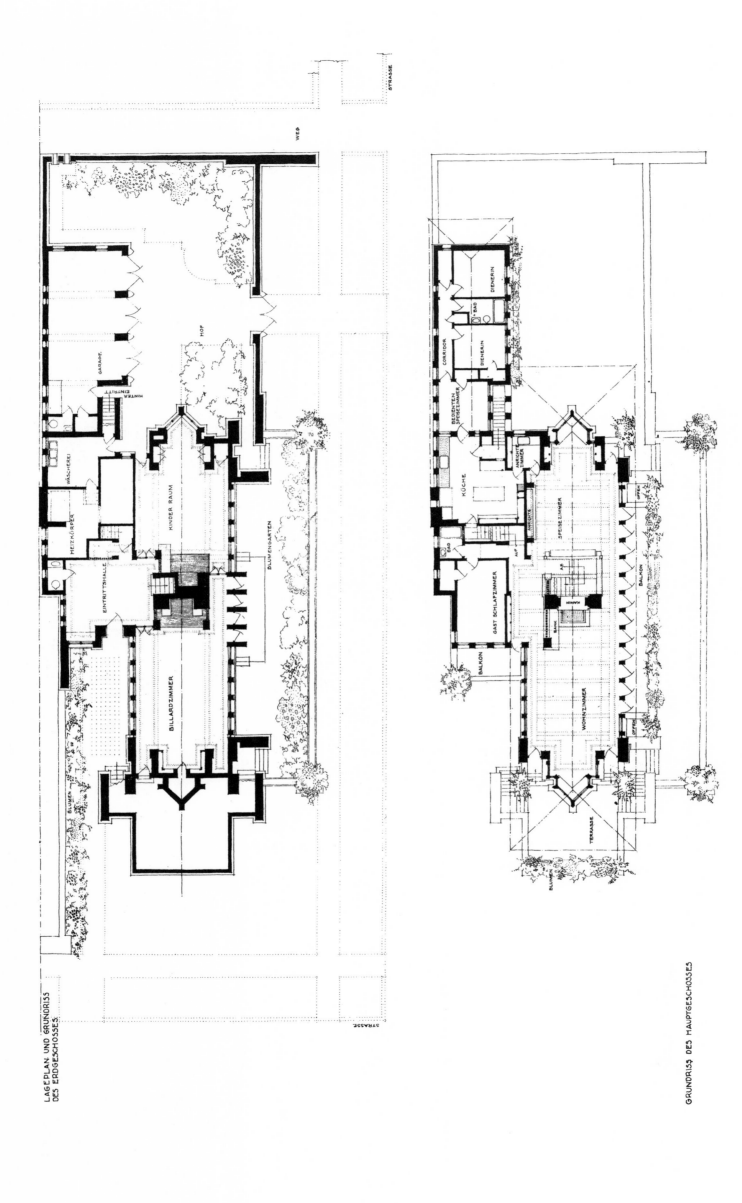

STRASSE

WEG

GARAGE

HINTER EINTRITT

WÄSCHEREI

HEIZKÖRPER

EINTRITTSHALLE

KINDER RAUM

HOF

BLUMENGARTEN

BILLARDZIMMER

BLUMEN

STRASSE

DIENERIN

BAD

DIENERIN

CORRIDOR

BEDIENTEN
SPEISEZIMMER

KÜCHE

ANRICHTE
ZIMMER

ANRICHTE

BAD

AUF

GAST SCHLAFZIMMER

SPEISE ZIMMER

KAMIN

BANK

BALKON

WOHNZIMMER

BALKON

OFFEN

OFFEN

BLUMEN

TERRASSE

GRUNDRISS DES HAUPTGESCHOSSES

PLATE xxxviii(b). Ground plan of the Robie house.

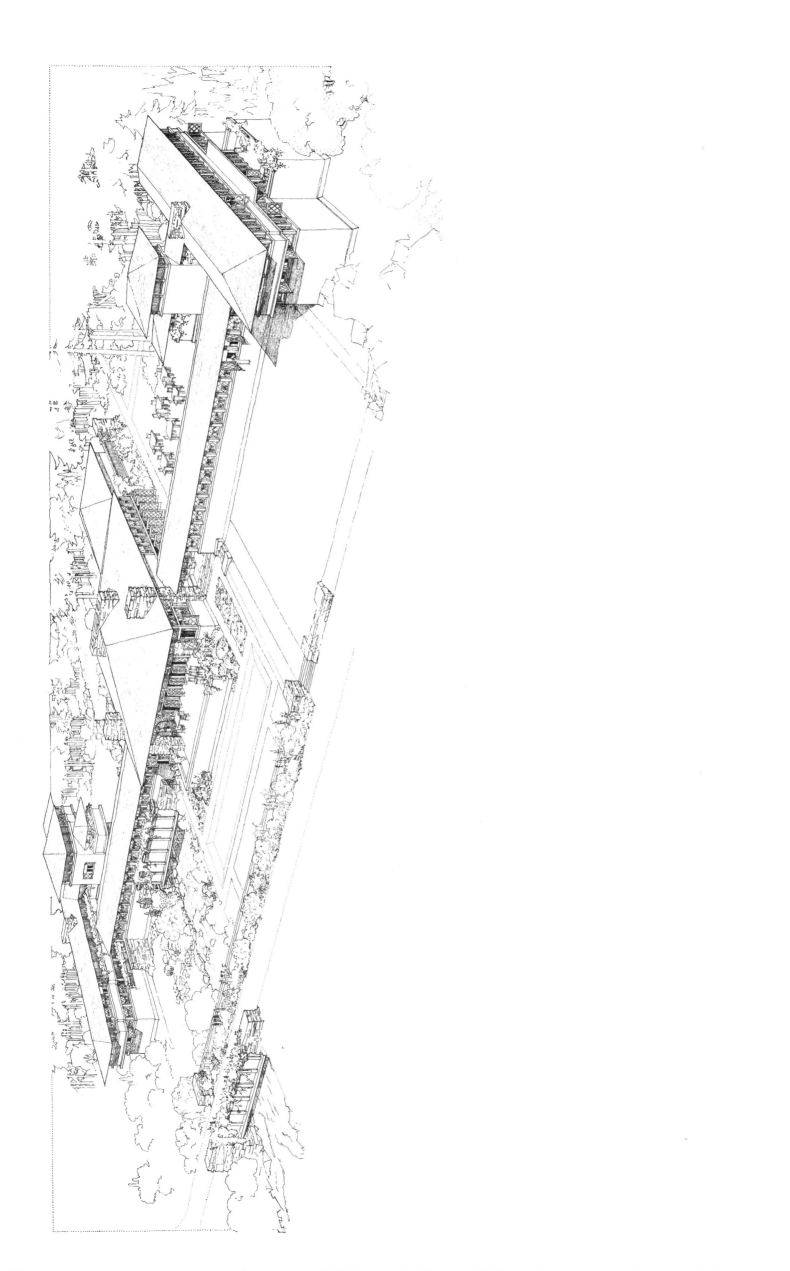

PLATE XXXVIII(a). Horse Shoe Inn, Estes Park, Colo.

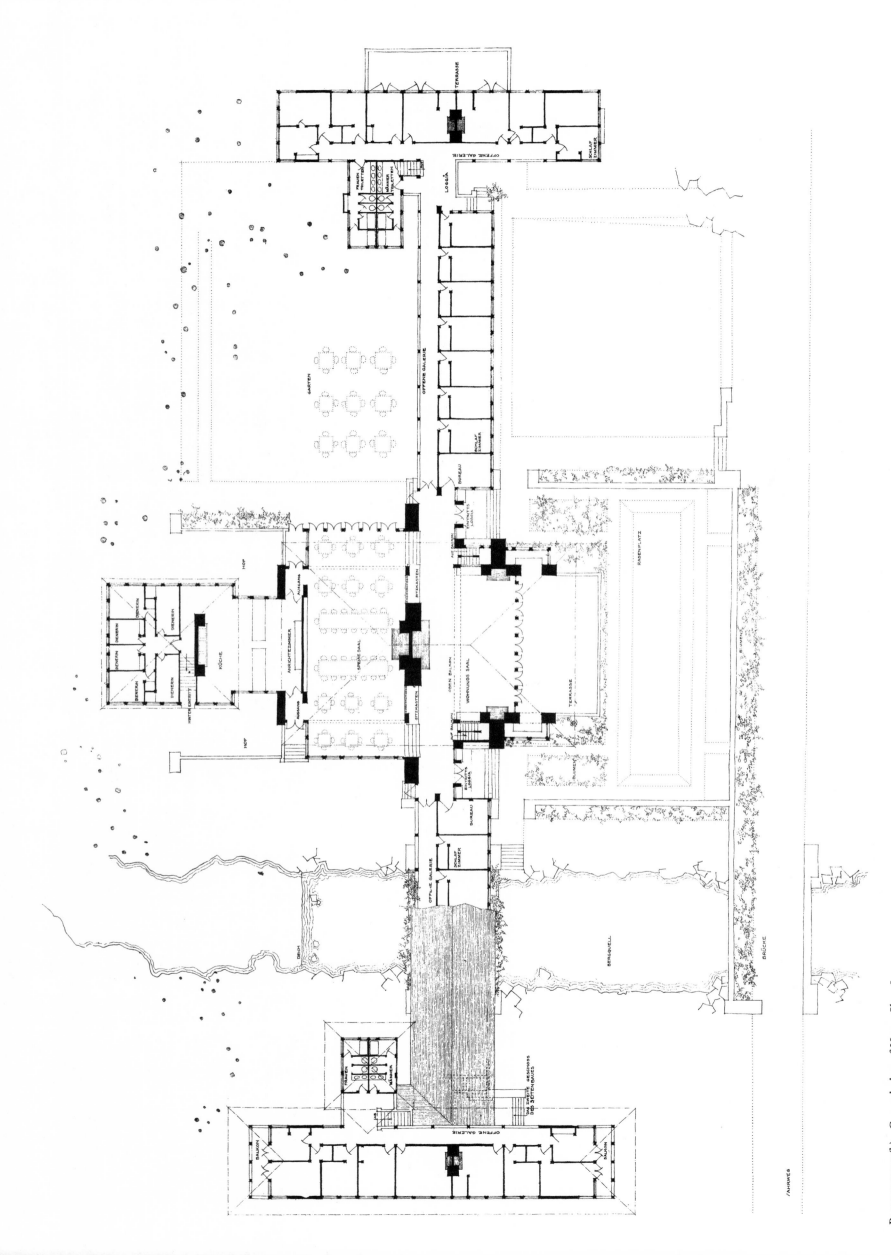

PLATE XXXVIII(b).   Ground plan of Horse Shoe Inn.

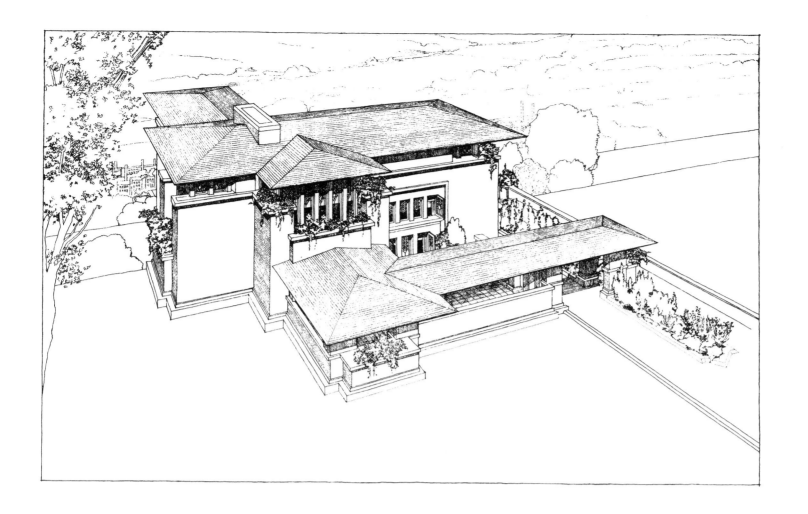

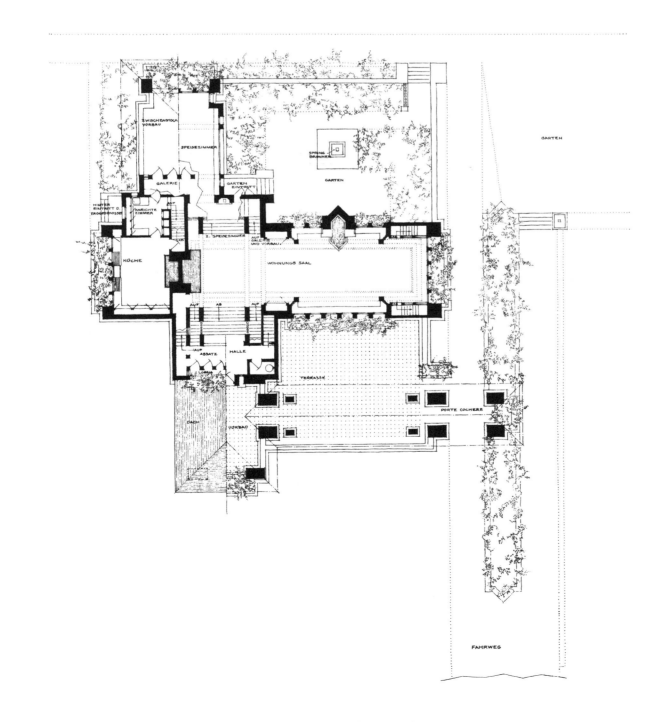

PLATE XXXIX. Suburban residence for Mr. Clark, Peoria, Ill. Perspective view and ground plan.

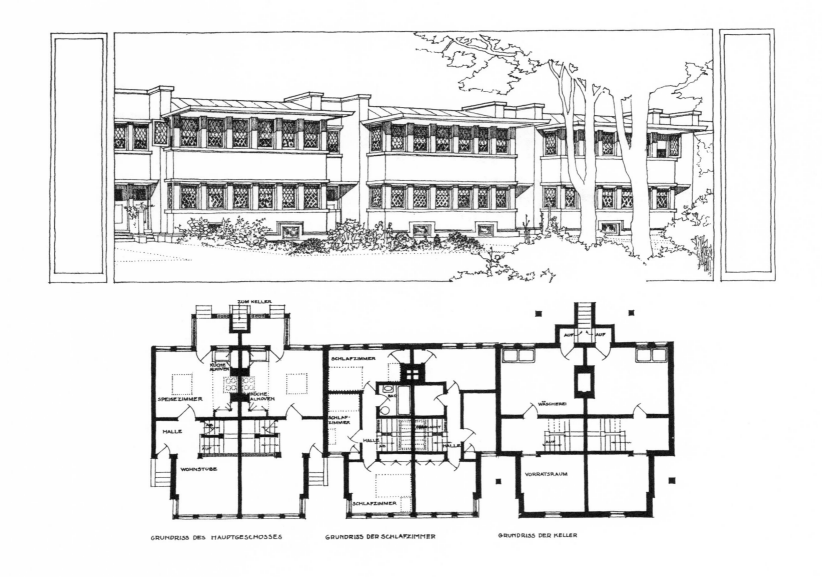

GRUNDRISS DES HAUPTGESCHOSSES   GRUNDRISS DER SCHLAFZIMMER   GRUNDRISS DER KELLER

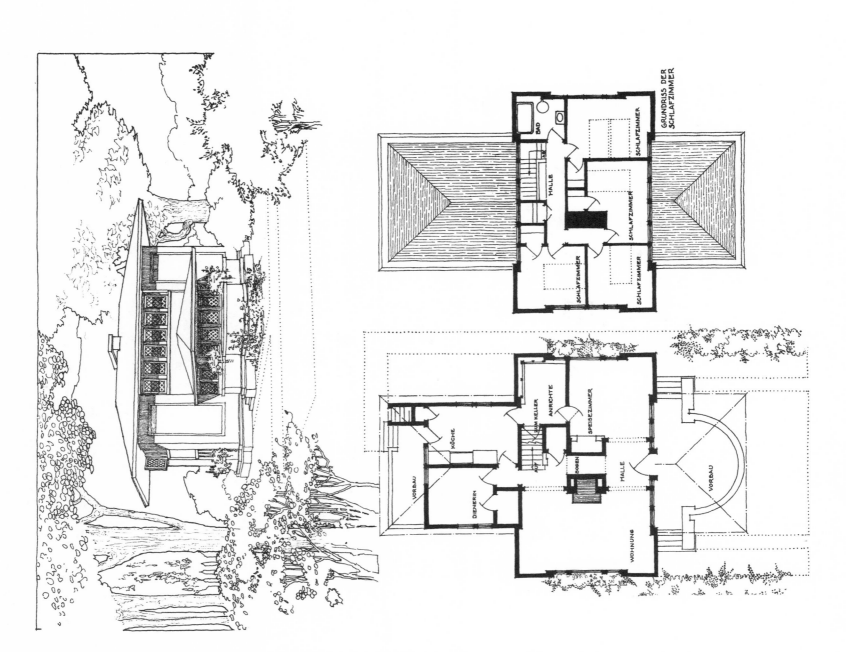

PLATE XL.   Workmen's cottages for Mr. E. C. Waller, Chicago, Ill. Suburban cottage for Miss Grace Fuller, Glencoe, Ill.

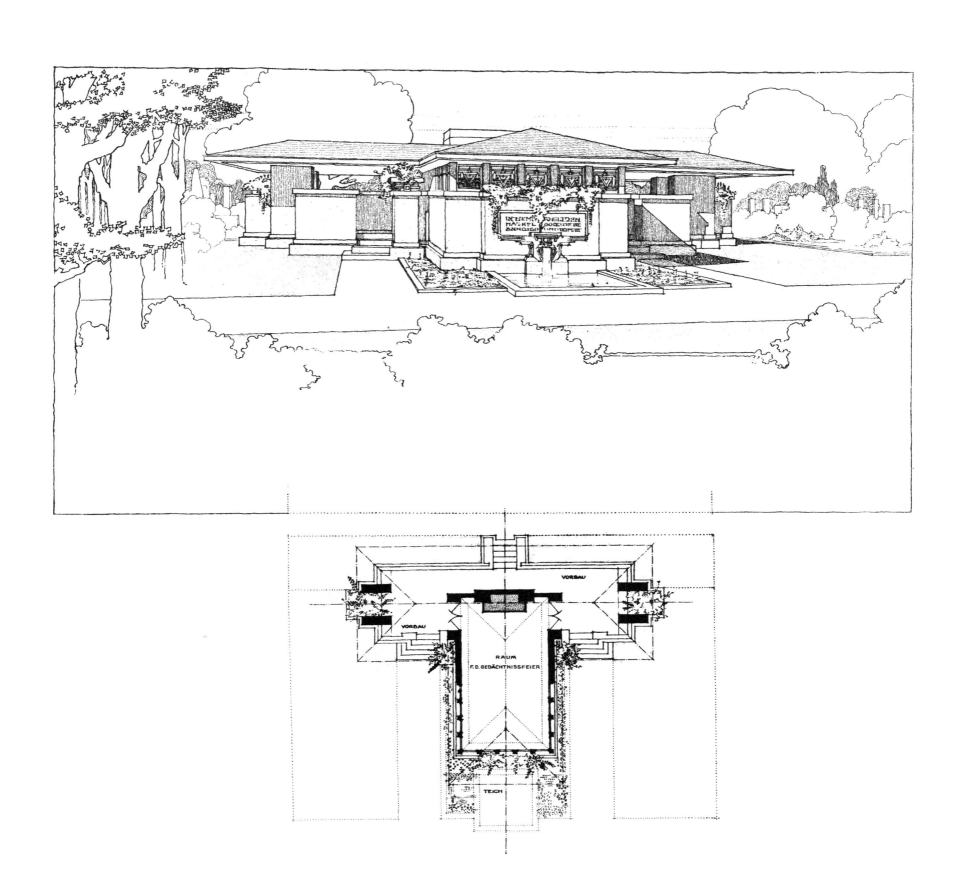

PLATE XLI. Pettit Memorial Chapel, Belvidere, Ill.

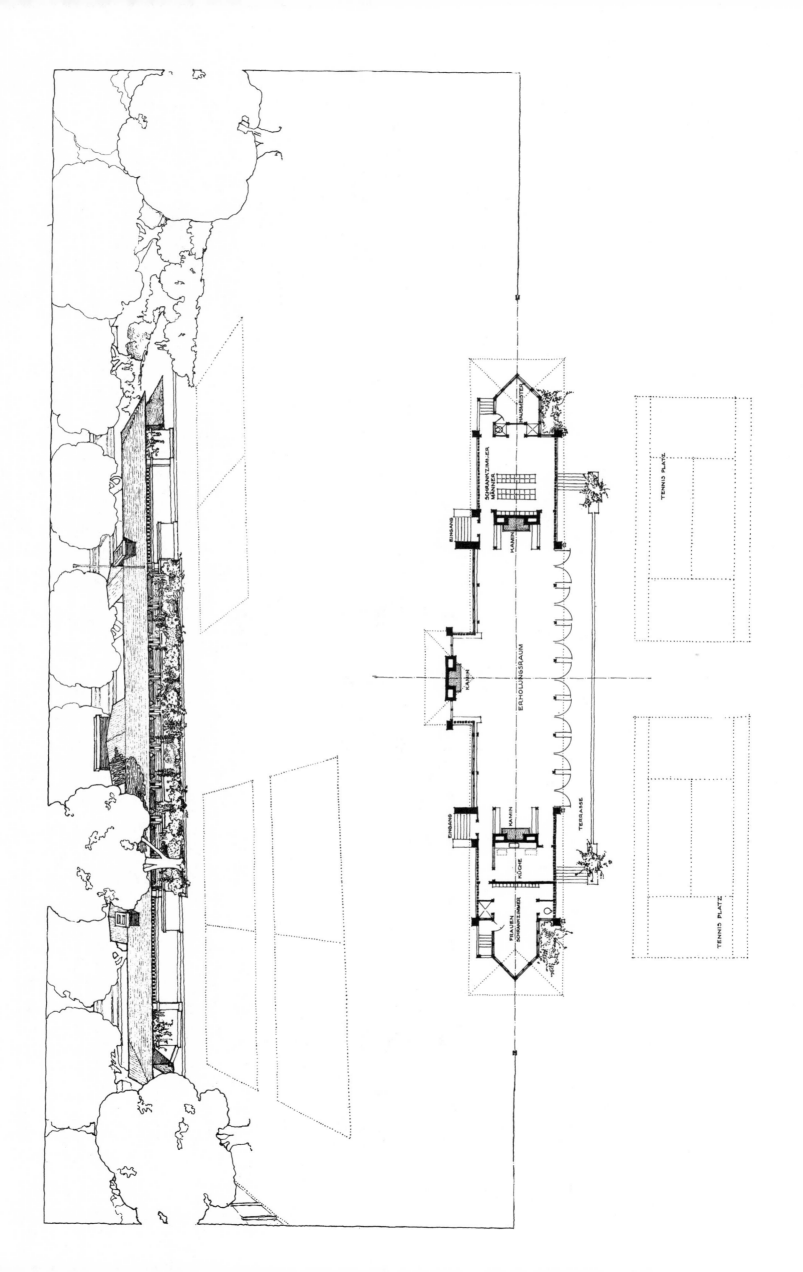

Plate XLII. River Forest Tennis Club, River Forest, Ill.

GRUNDRISS DES HAUPTGESCHOSSES

FAHRWEG

BIBLIOTHEK

TERRASSE

KÜCHE

WOHNZIMMER

GARDEROBE

KORRIDOR

SCHLAFZIMMER

BAD

ANKLEIDE

ANKLEIDE

SCHLAFZIMMER

VERANDA

BRÜCKE

PAVILLON

BACH

PLATE XLIII(a). House for Mr. Glasner in a suburb of Glencoe, Ill.

PLATE XLIII(b). Summer house in Fresno, Calif. Suburban house in Highland Park, Ill.

PLATE XLIV. Suburban dwelling for George E. Millard, Highland Park, Ill.

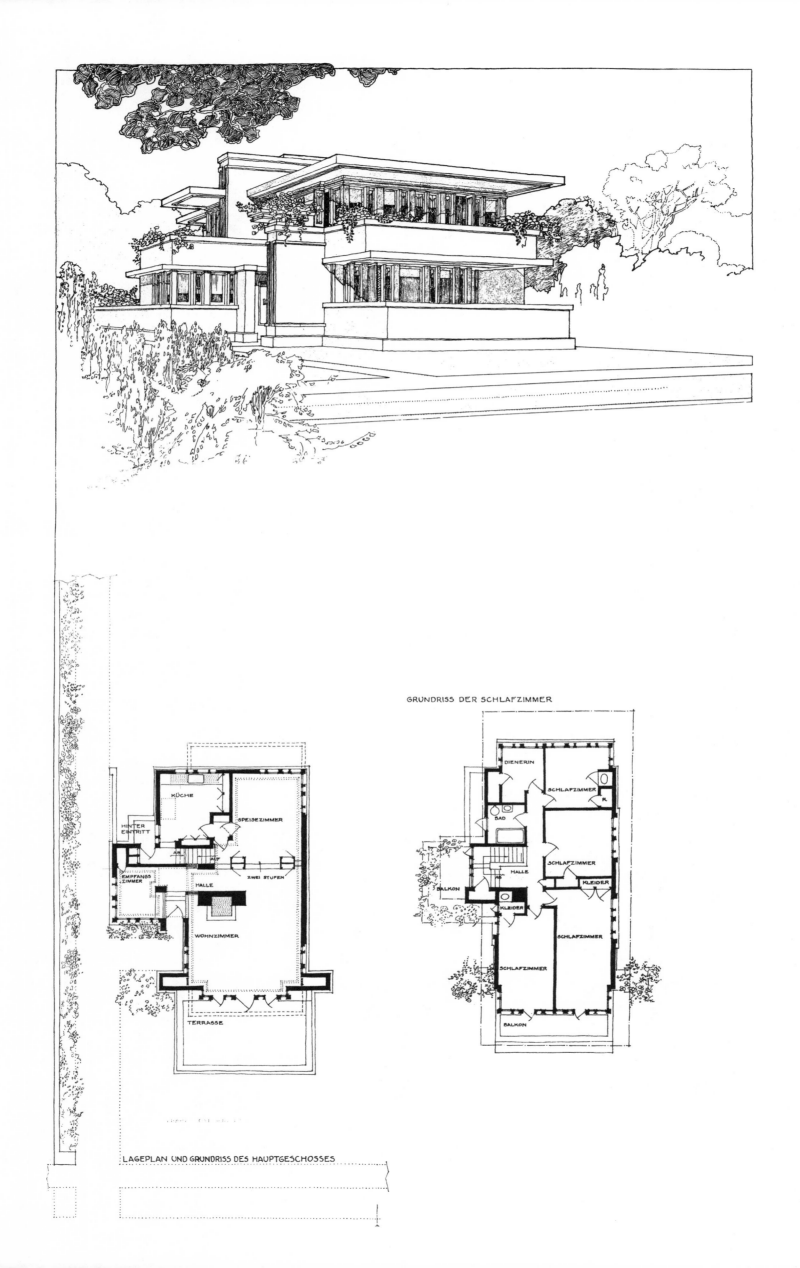

GRUNDRISS DER SCHLAFZIMMER

KÜCHE

SPEISEZIMMER

HINTER
EINTRITT

EMPFANGS
ZIMMER

ZWEI STUFEN

HALLE

WOHNZIMMER

TERRASSE

DIENERIN

SCHLAFZIMMER

BAD

SCHLAFZIMMER

BALKON

HALLE

KLEIDER

KLEIDER

SCHLAFZIMMER

SCHLAFZIMMER

BALKON

LAGEPLAN UND GRUNDRISS DES HAUPTGESCHOSSES

PLATE XLV. Cottage for Mrs. Thomas H. Gale, Oak Park, Ill.

PLATE XLVI(a). General perspective view of Como Orchard Summer Colony.

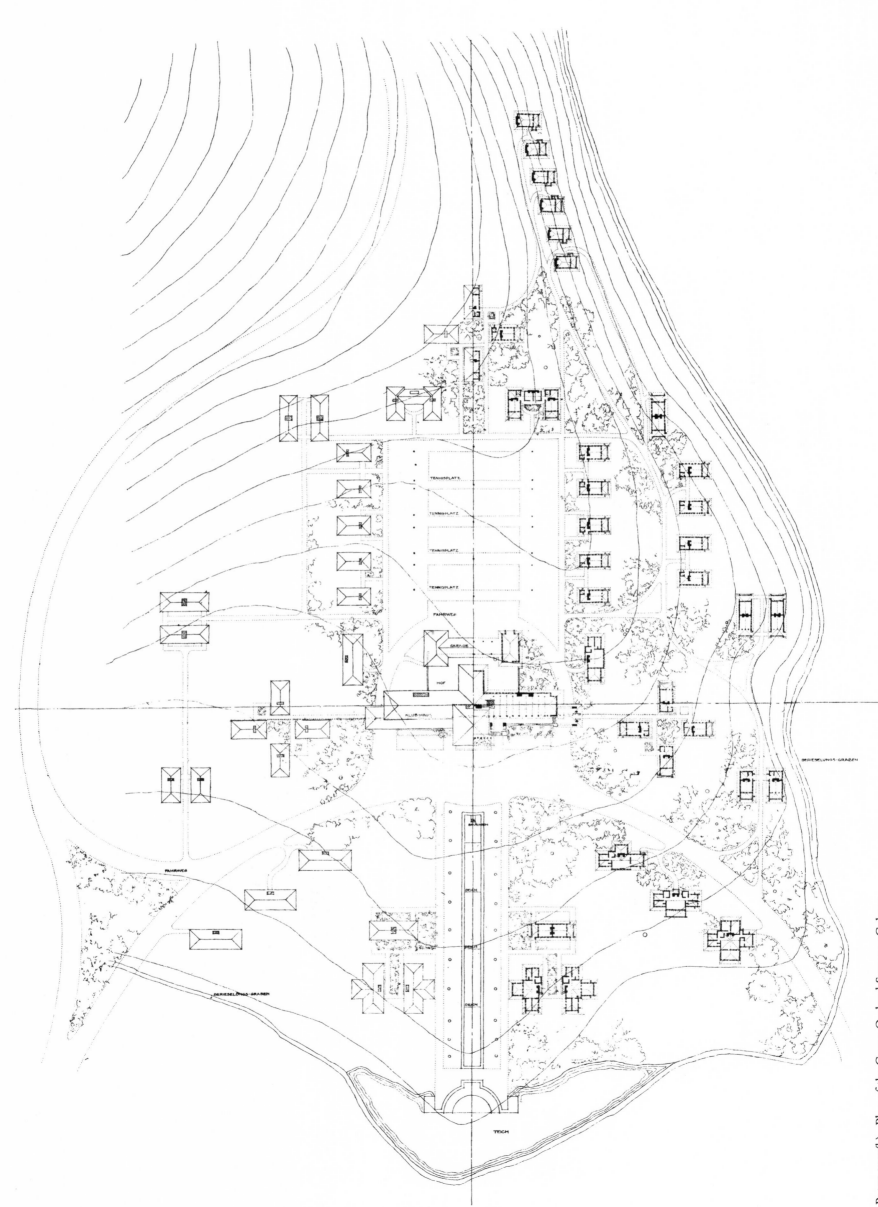

PLATE XLVI(b). Plan of the Como Orchard Summer Colony.

PLATE XLVII(a). Central club house for the Como Orchard Summer Colony.

PLATE XLVII(b). Typical cottages, Como Orchard Summer Colony.

PLATE xlviii(a). Three typical houses for real-estate subdivision for Mr. E. C. Waller.

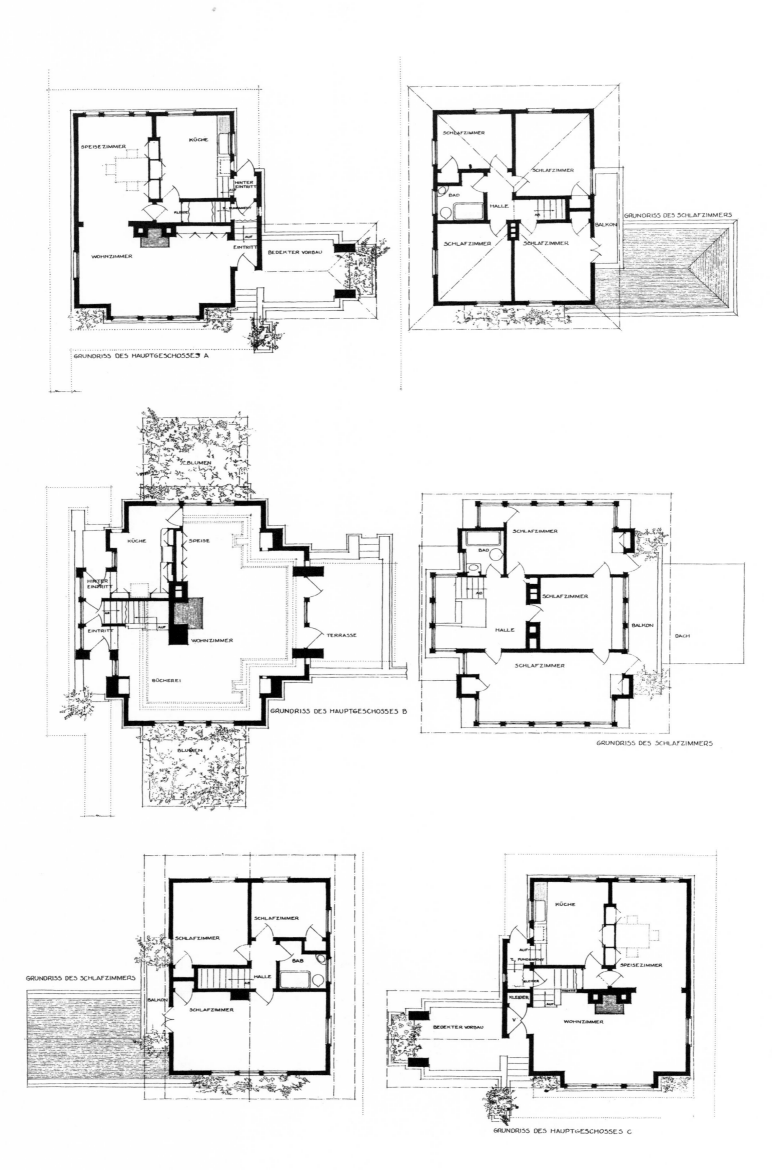

SPEISEZIMMER KÜCHE
HINTER EINTRITT
KLEIDER
AUF
WOHNZIMMER EINTRITT BEDEKTER VORBAU
BALKON

GRUNDRISS DES HAUPTGESCHOSSES A

SCHLAFZIMMER
SCHLAFZIMMER
BAD HALLE AB
SCHLAFZIMMER SCHLAFZIMMER BALKON

GRUNDRISS DES SCHLAFZIMMERS

BLUMEN
KÜCHE SPEISE
HINTER EINTRITT
AUF
AB
EINTRITT WOHNZIMMER TERRASSE
BÜCHEREI
GRUNDRISS DES HAUPTGESCHOSSES B
BLUMEN

SCHLAFZIMMER
BAD
SCHLAFZIMMER
AB
HALLE BALKON DACH
SCHLAFZIMMER

GRUNDRISS DES SCHLAFZIMMERS

SCHLAFZIMMER
SCHLAFZIMMER
BAB
GRUNDRISS DES SCHLAFZIMMERS HALLE
BALKON SCHLAFZIMMER

KÜCHE
AUF
FUNDAMENT SPEISEZIMMER
KLEIDER AB
BEDEKTER VORBAU KLEIDER AUF
V WOHNZIMMER

GRUNDRISS DES HAUPTGESCHOSSES C

PLATE XLVIII(b). Ground plans for the three houses for Mr. E. C. Waller.

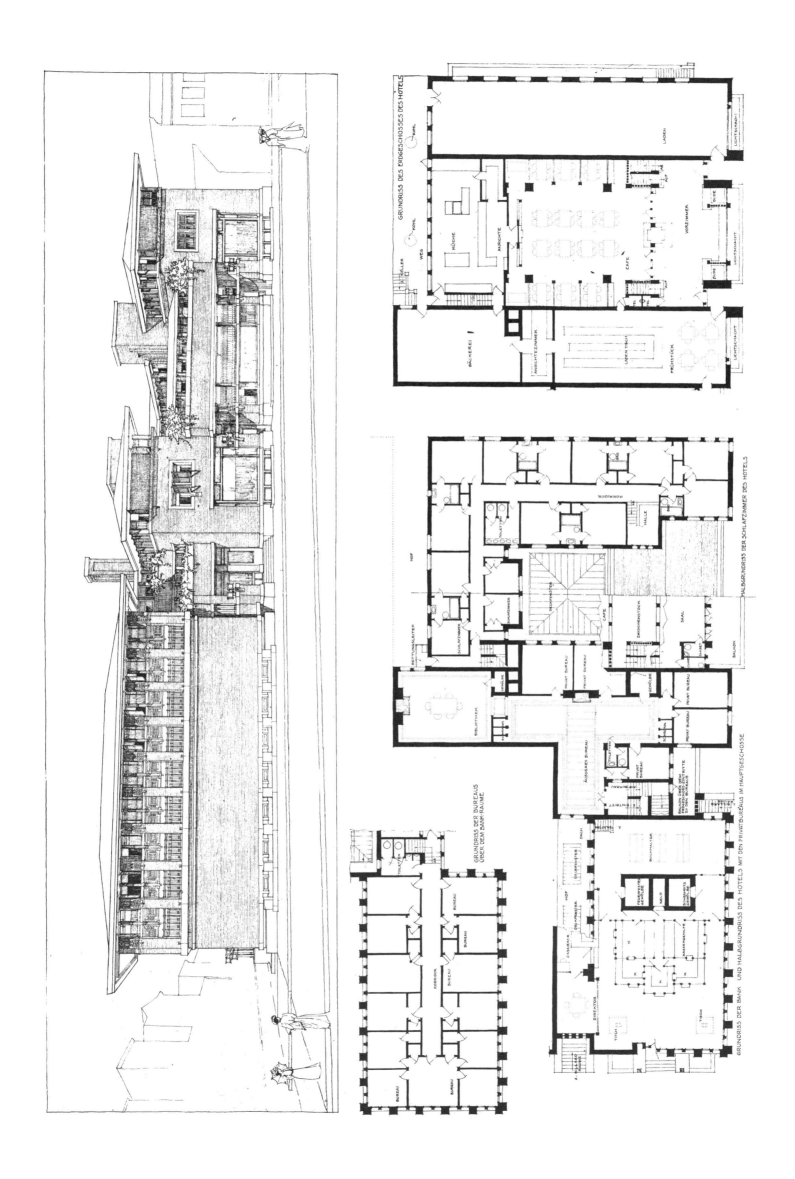

PLATE XLIX(a). Bank and office building for the City National Bank, Mason City, Io.

PLATE XLIX(b). View of the bank and office building for the City National Bank.

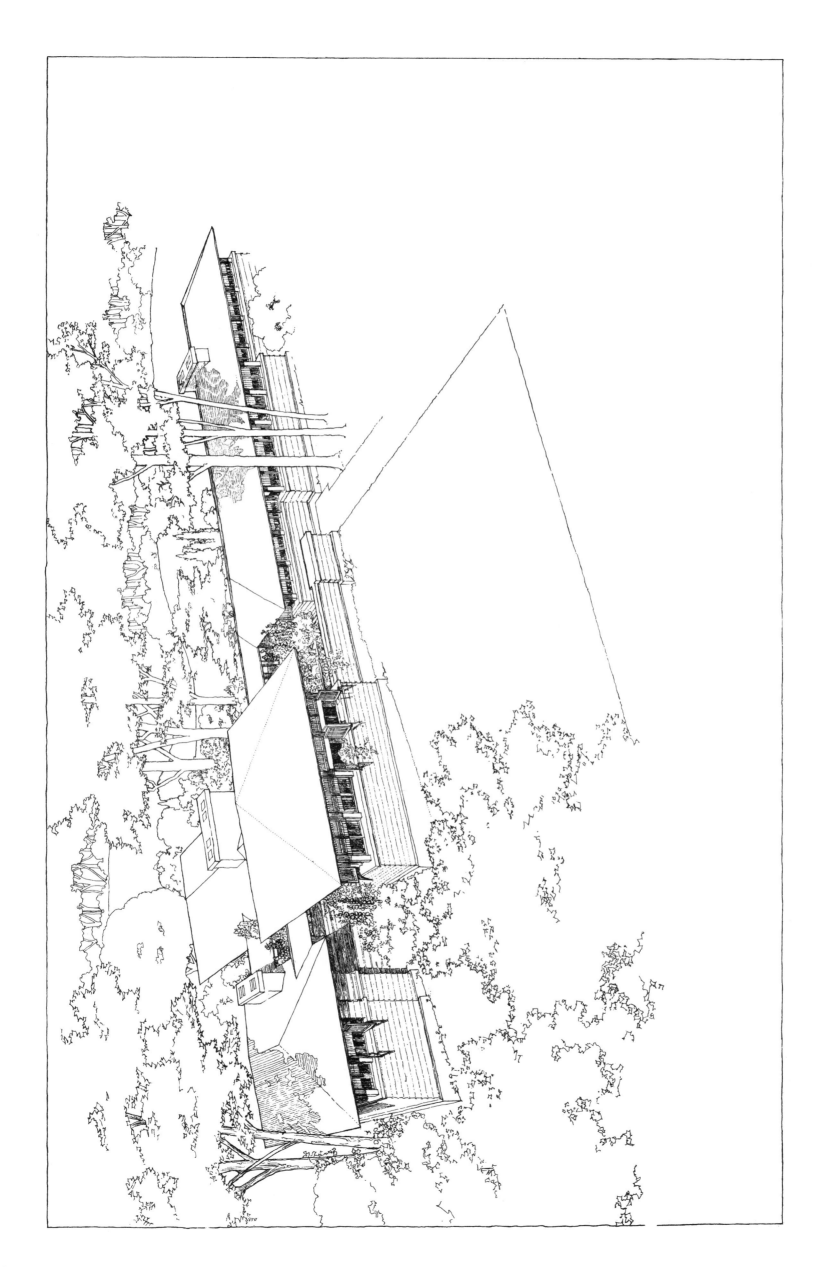

PLATE L. Cottage for Elizabeth Stone, Glencoe, Ill.

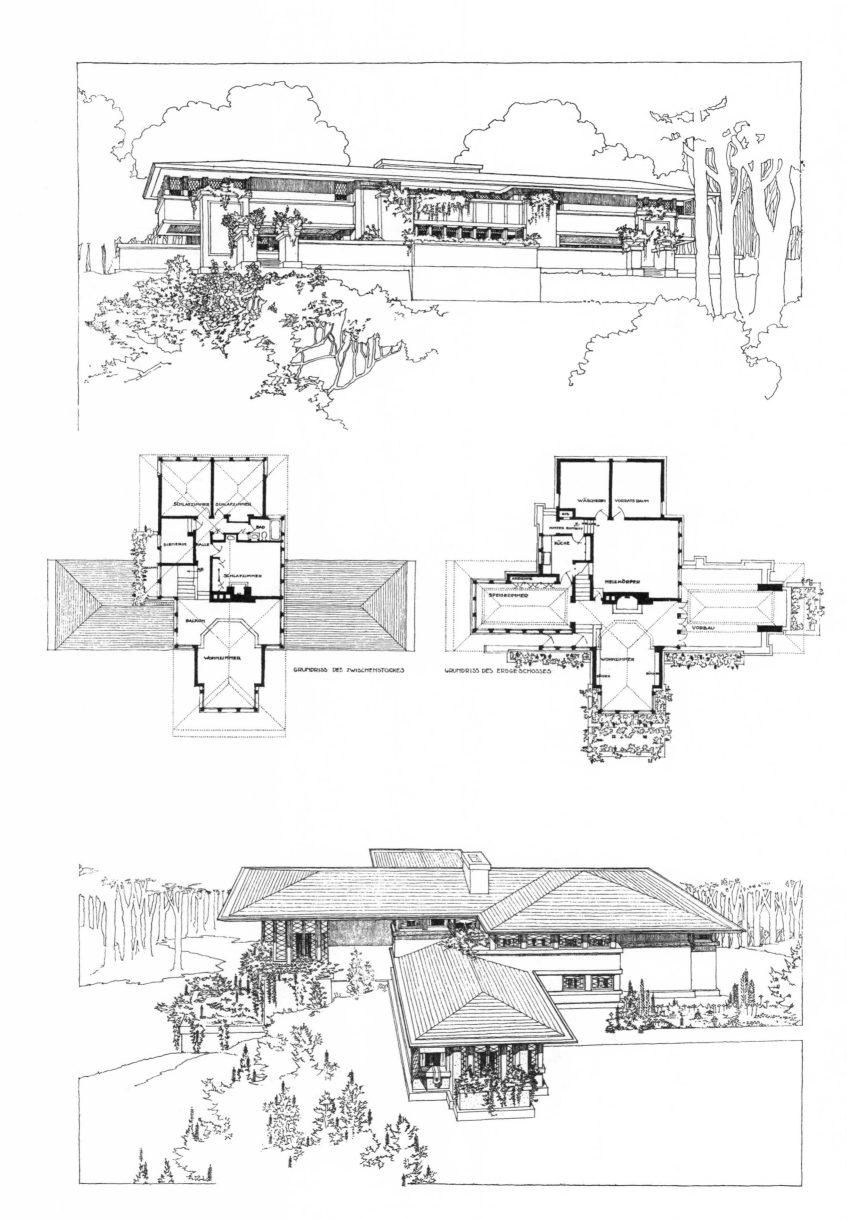

Labels within floor plans (left plan):
SCHLAFZIMMER SCHLAFZIMMER
DIENERIN HALLE BAD
SCHLAFZIMMER
BALKON
WOHNZIMMER
GRUNDRISS DES ZWISCHENSTOCKES

Labels within floor plans (right plan):
WÄSCHEREI VORRATS RAUM
HINTER EINTRITT
KÜCHE
ARBEITE
SPEISEZIMMER HEIZKÖRPER
VORBAU
WOHNZIMMER
GRUNDRISS DES ERDGESCHOSSES

PLATE LI. Ground plan and perspective view for the house of Isabel Roberts, River Forest, Ill.
Study for a summer house for Mr. E. E. Waller, Charlevoix, Mich.

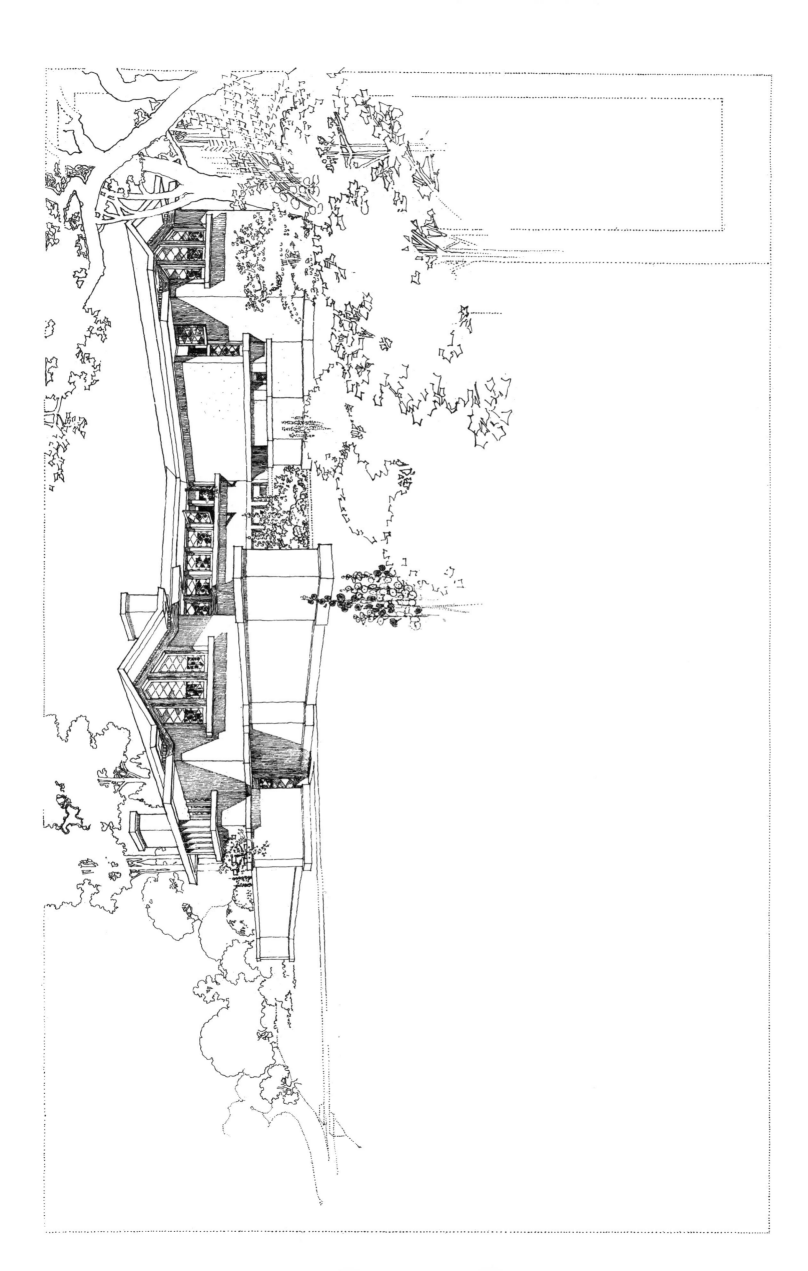

PLATE LIII(a). Home for Walter Gerts at Glencoe, Ill.

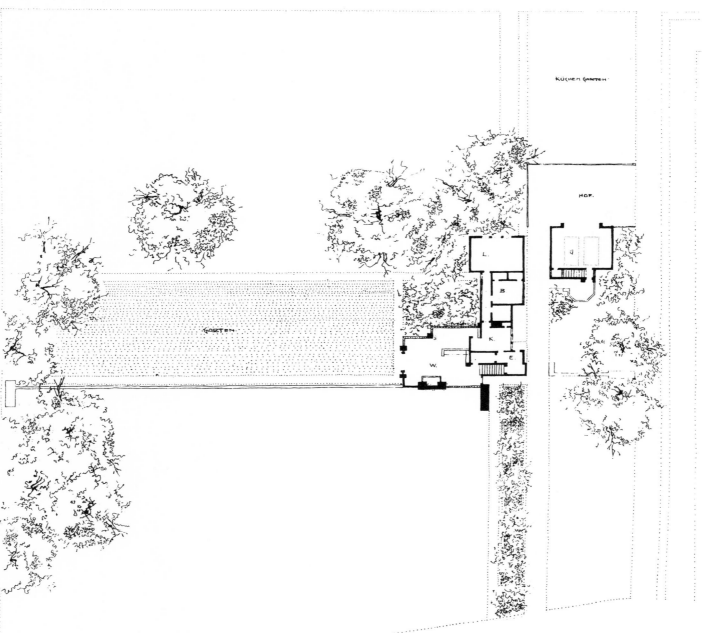

PLATE LII(b). Home for Walter Gerts.

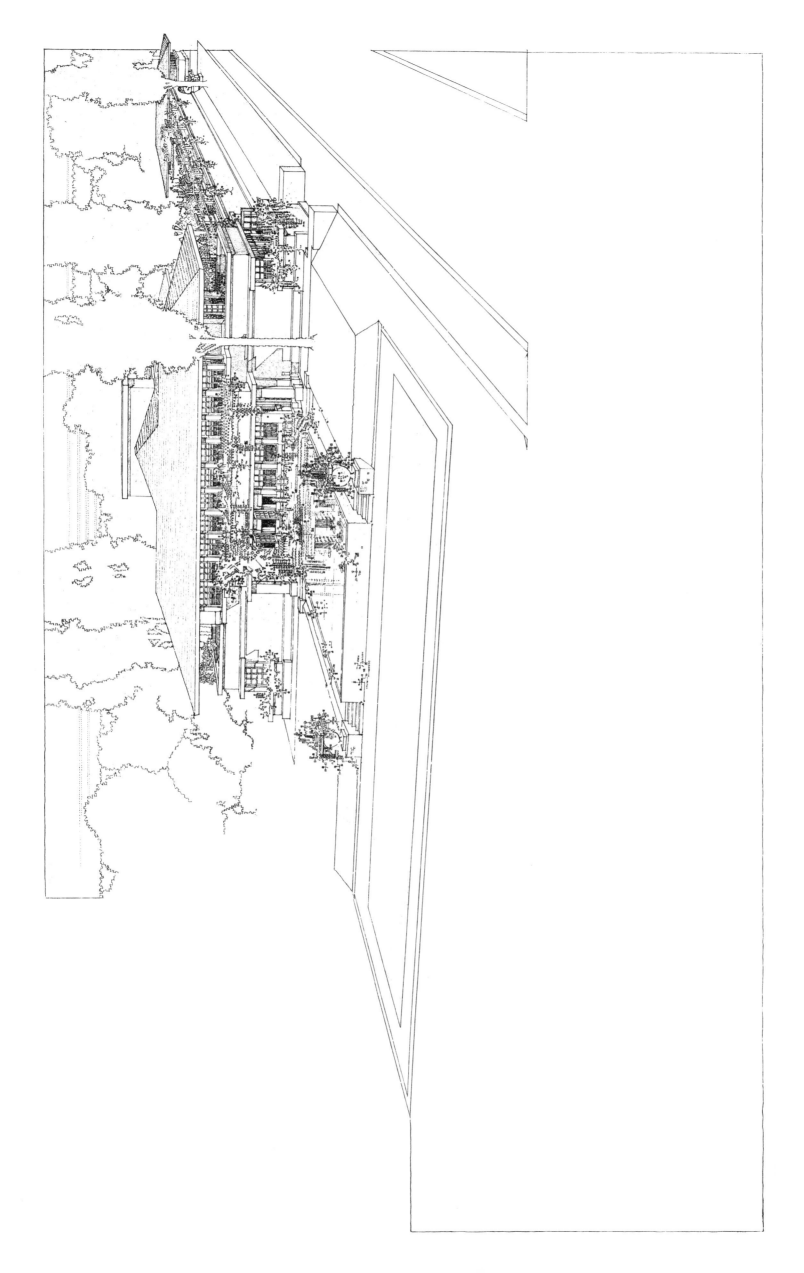

PLATE LIII(a). Home of Burton S. Westcott, Springfield, Oh.

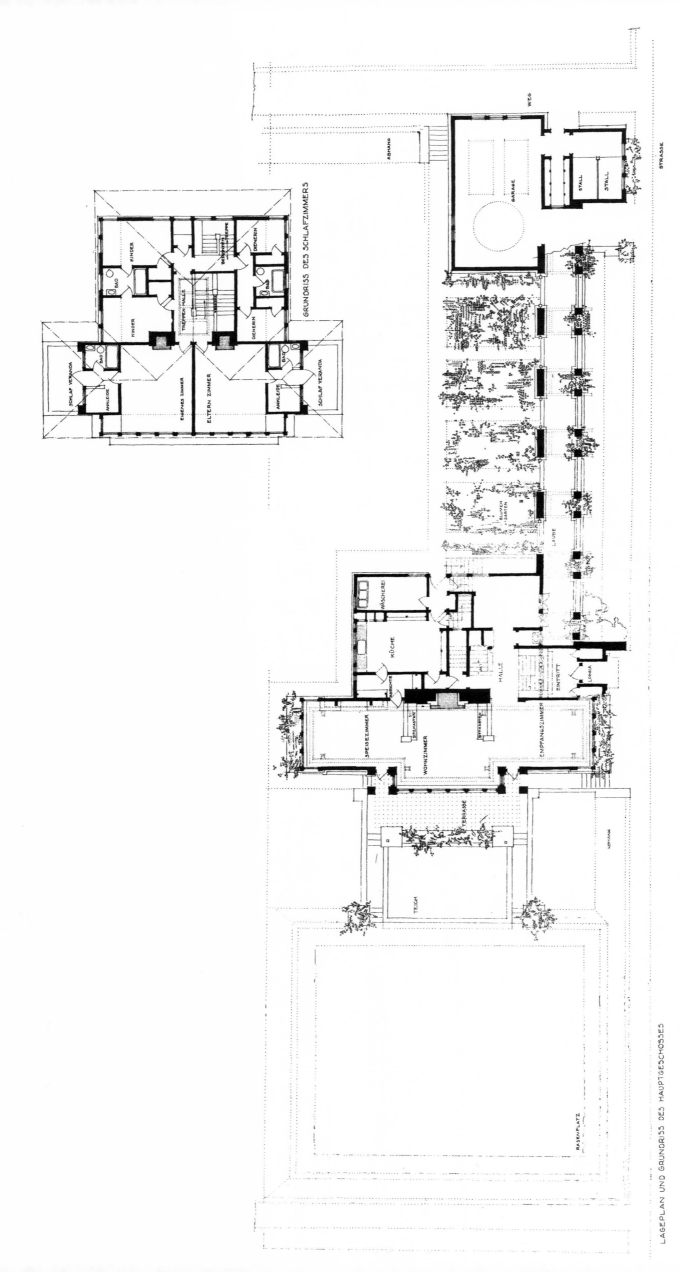

PLATE LIII(b). Ground plan, Burton S. Westcott house.

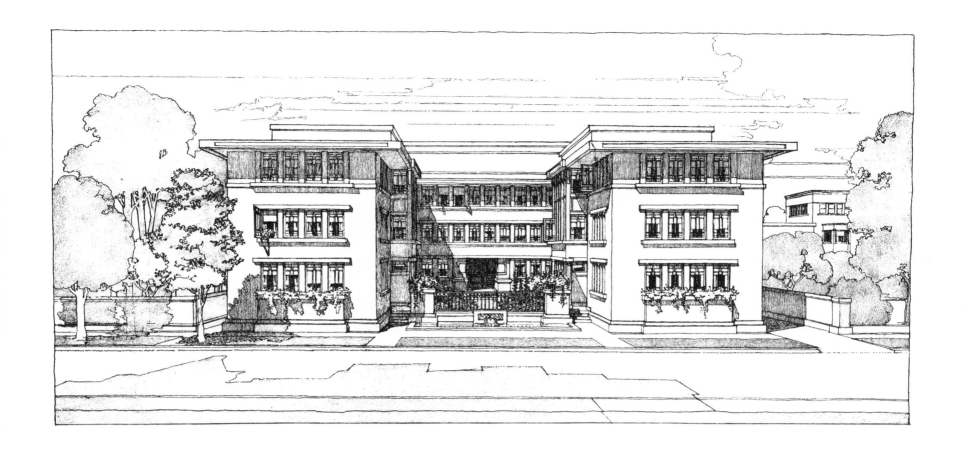

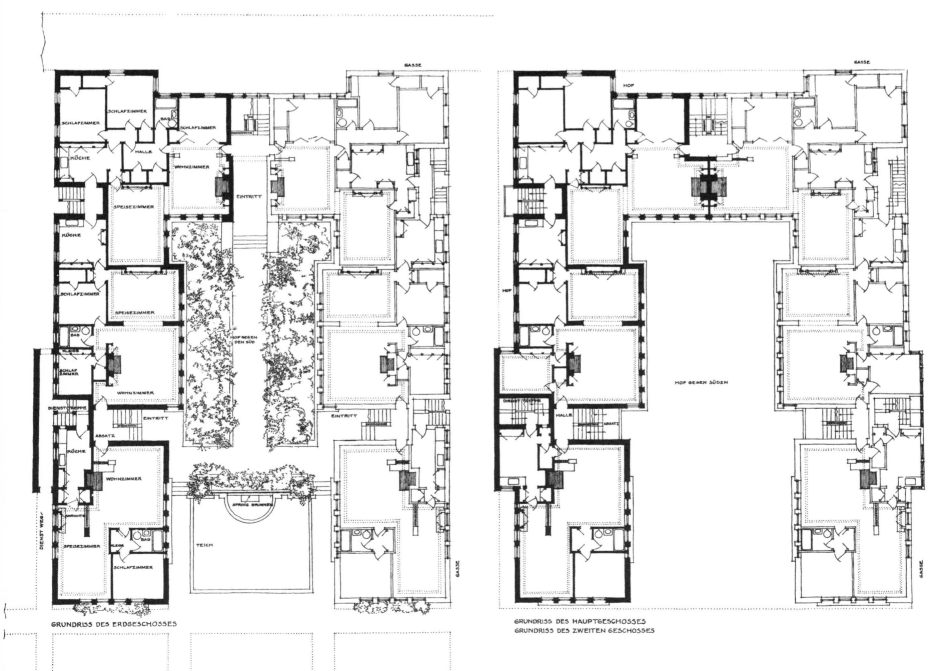

GRUNDRISS DES ERDGESCHOSSES

GRUNDRISS DES HAUPTGESCHOSSES
GRUNDRISS DES ZWEITEN GESCHOSSES

PLATE LIV. Concrete flat building at Kenwood for Warren McArthur, Chicago, Ill

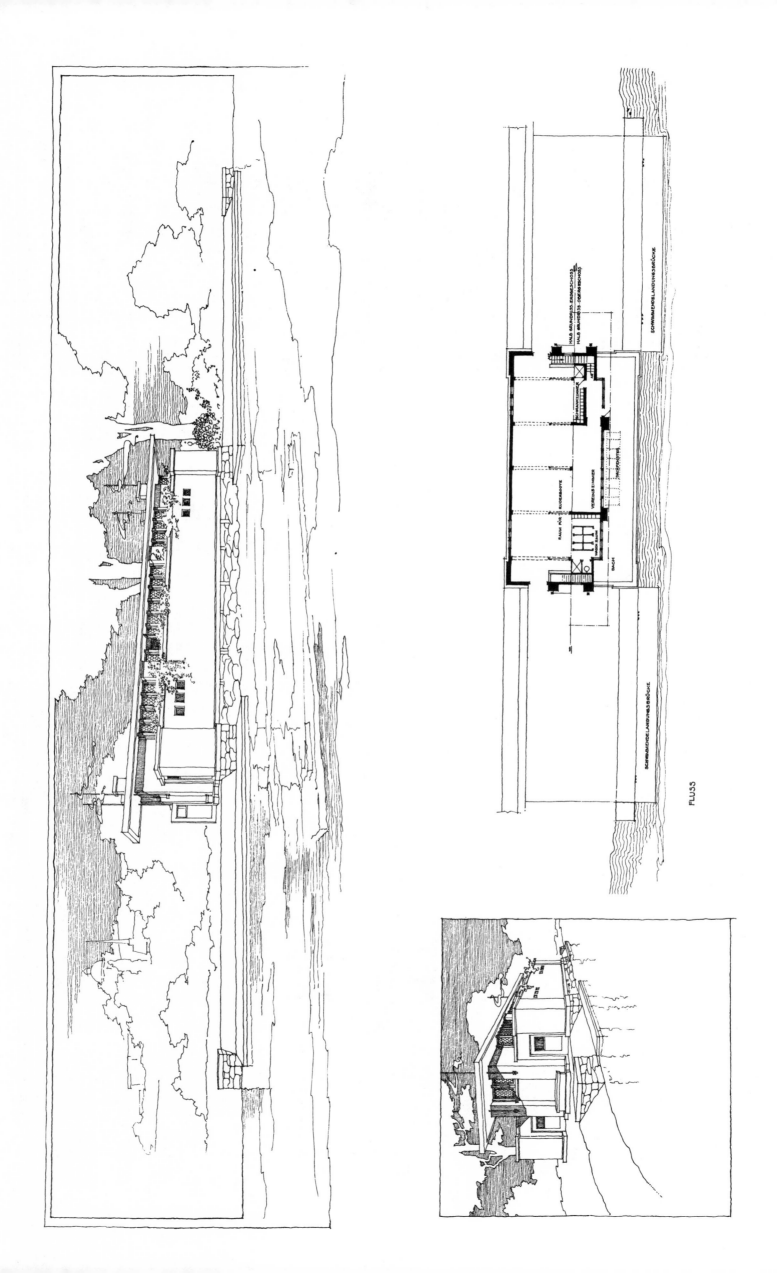

SCHWIMMSCHULANDUNGSBRÜCKE
HALB GRUNDRISS. ERDGESCHOSS
HALB GRUNDRISS. OBERGESCHOSS
SCHWIMMSCHULANDUNGSBRÜCKE
RAUM FÜR RUDERBOOTE
SCHRANKZIMMER
VEREINS ZIMMER
ZIMMERVORMT.
RUDER BAUM
DACH
FLUSS

PLATE LV.   Boathouse for the University of Wisconsin Boat Club.

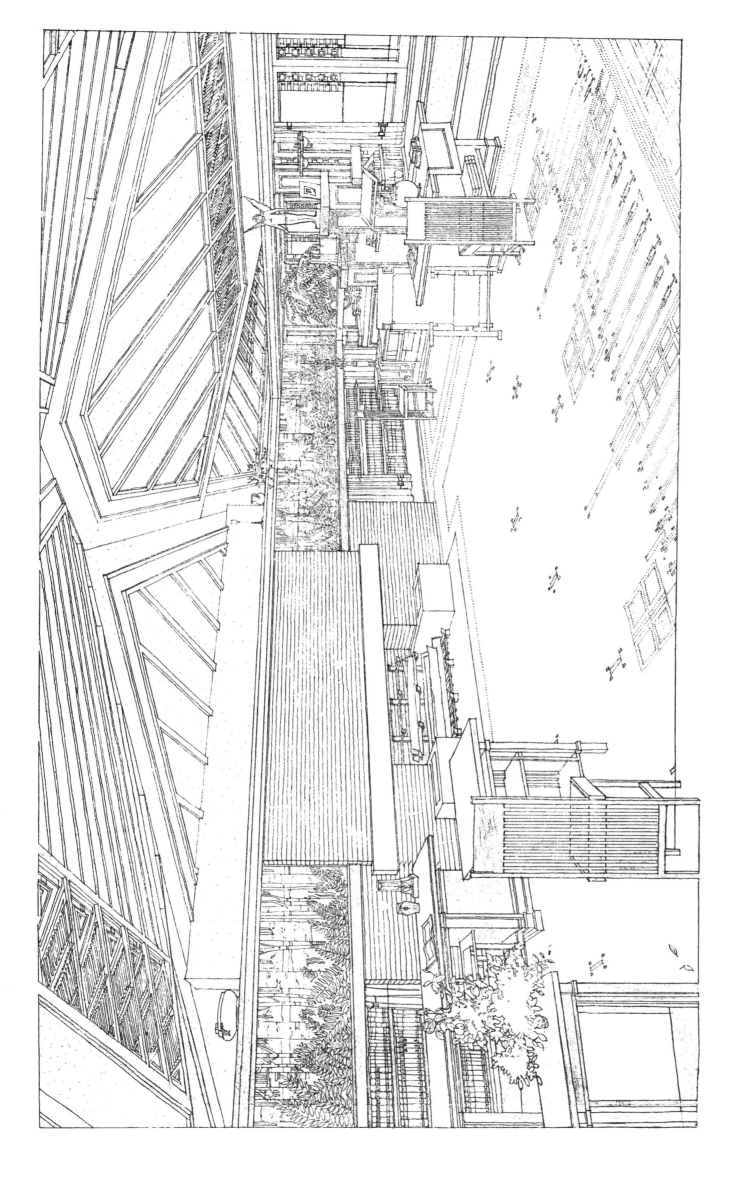

PLATE LVI(a). Living-room interior, dwelling for Mr. and Mrs. Avery Coonley, Riverside, Ill.

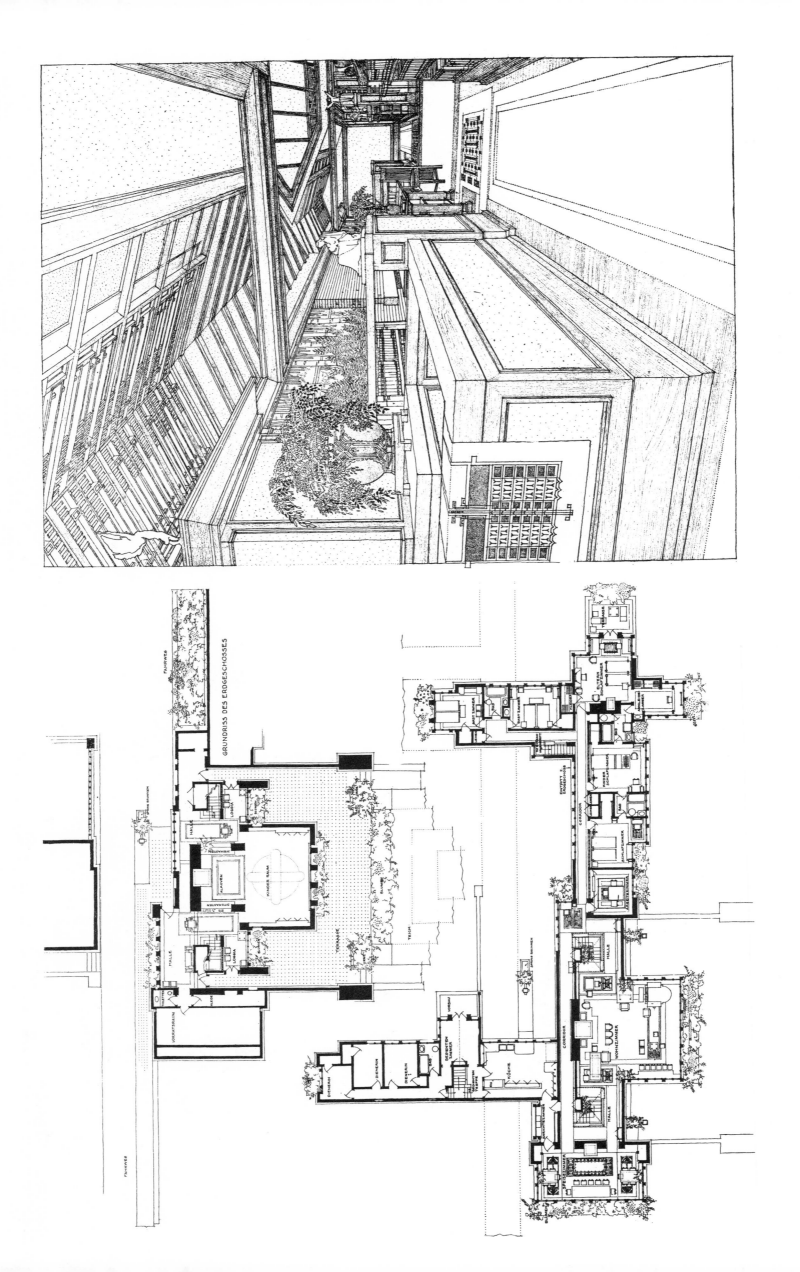

PLATE LVI(b). Ground plan and view of entrance alcove, the Coonley house.

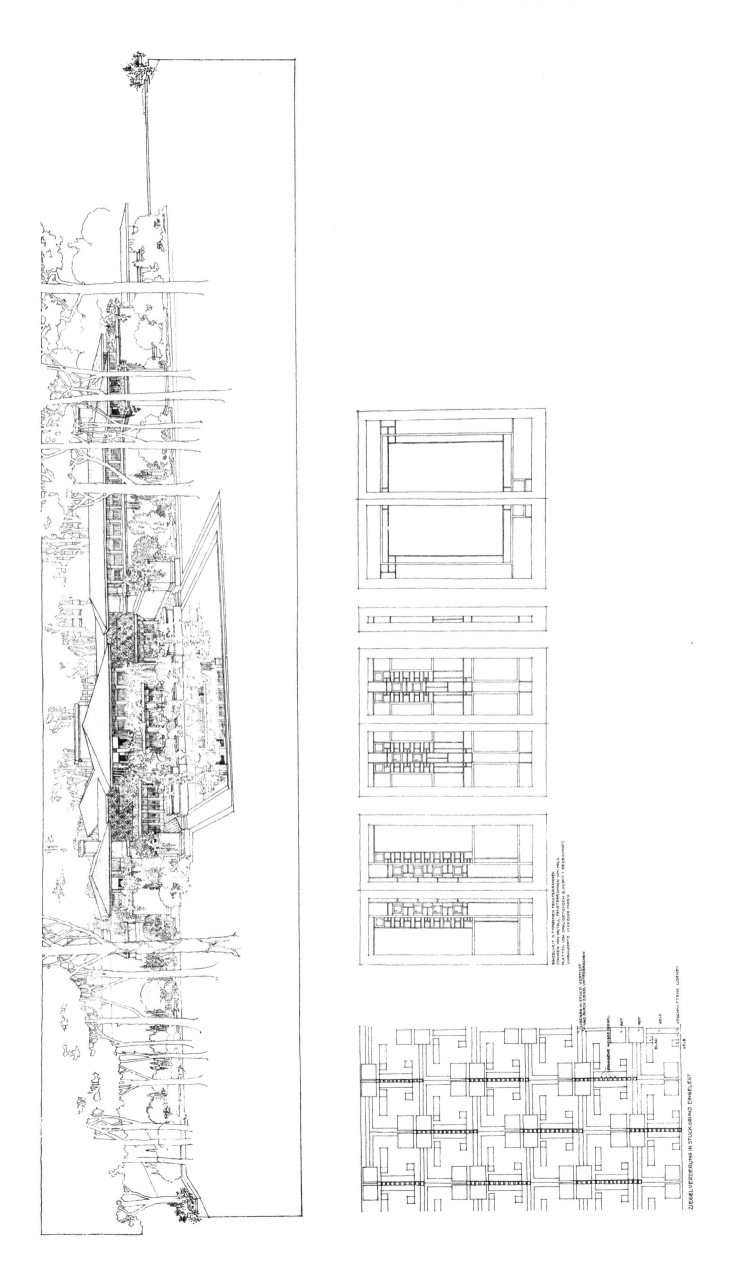

PLATE LVII(a). The Coonley house.

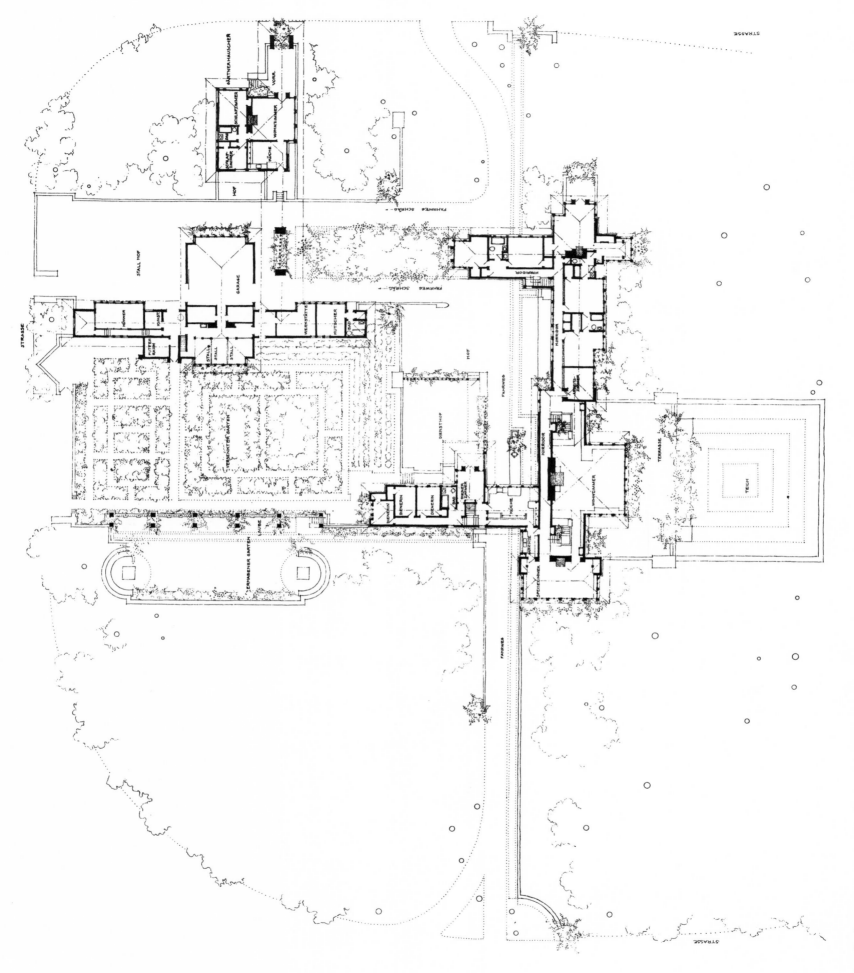

PLATE LVII(b). Ground plan, Coonley house.

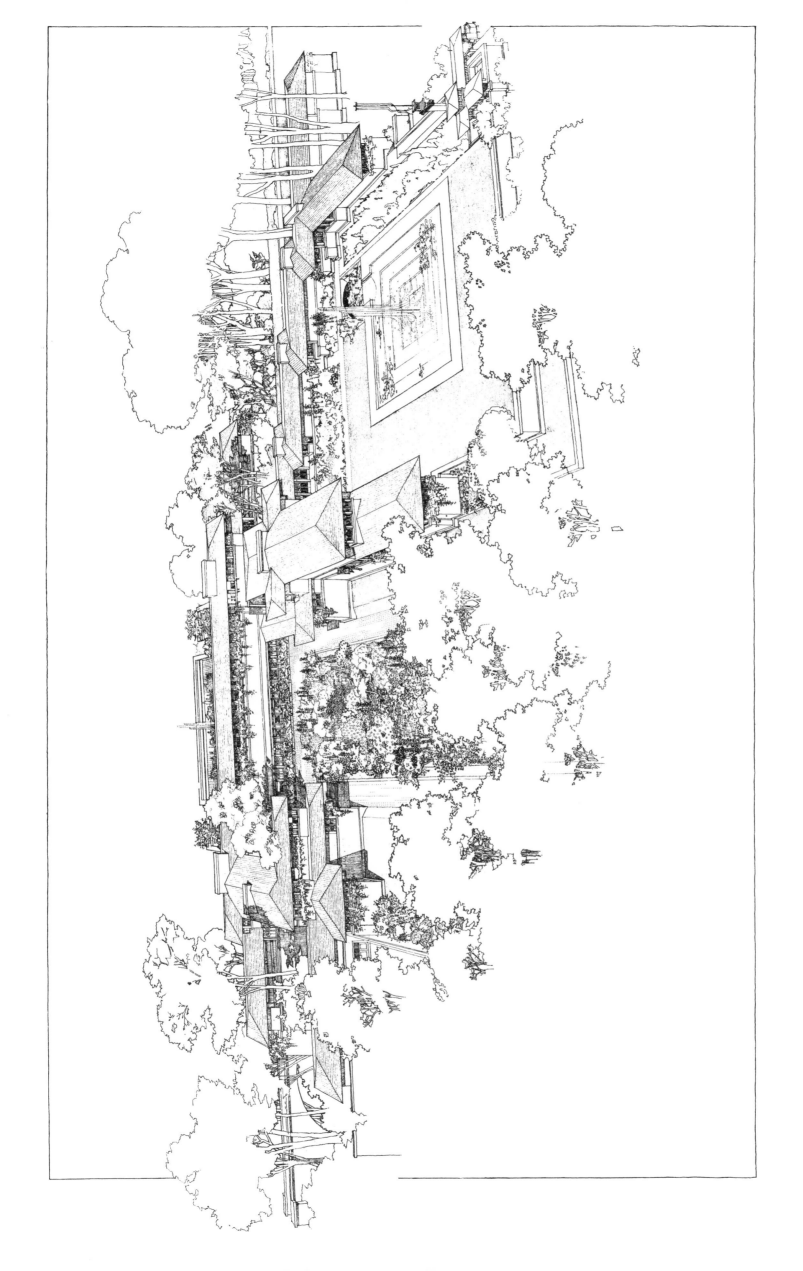

PLATE LVIII(a). Design for summer residence of Harold McCormick, at Lake Forest.

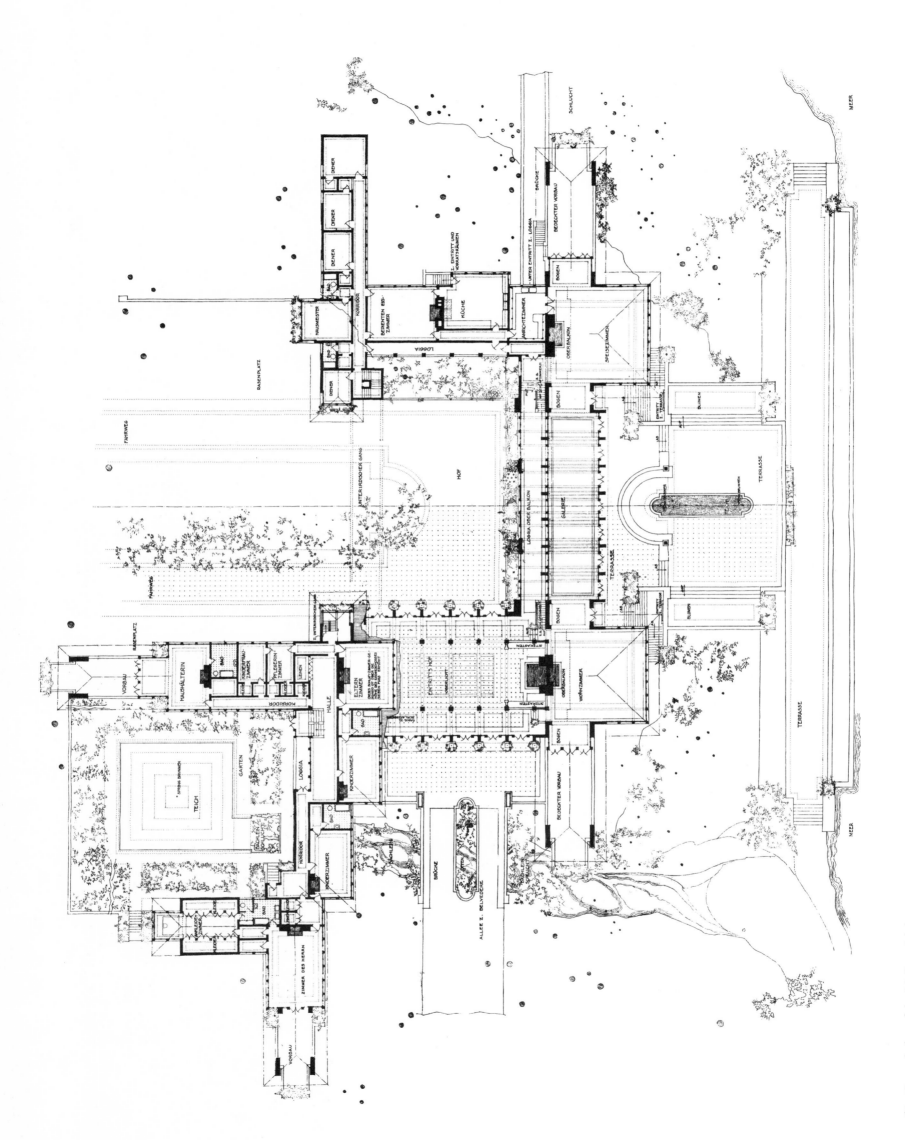

PLATE LVIII(b). Ground plan of the McCormick house.

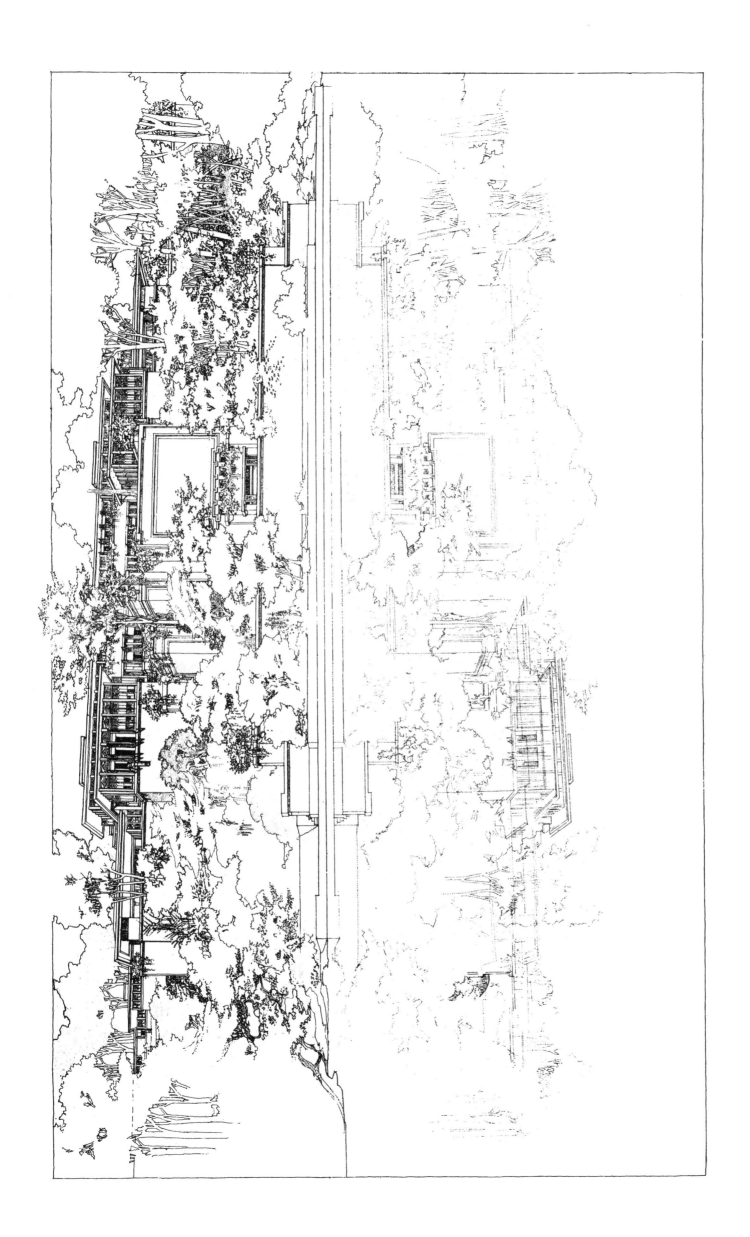

PLATE LIX. Summer residence of Harold McCormick, from the lake.

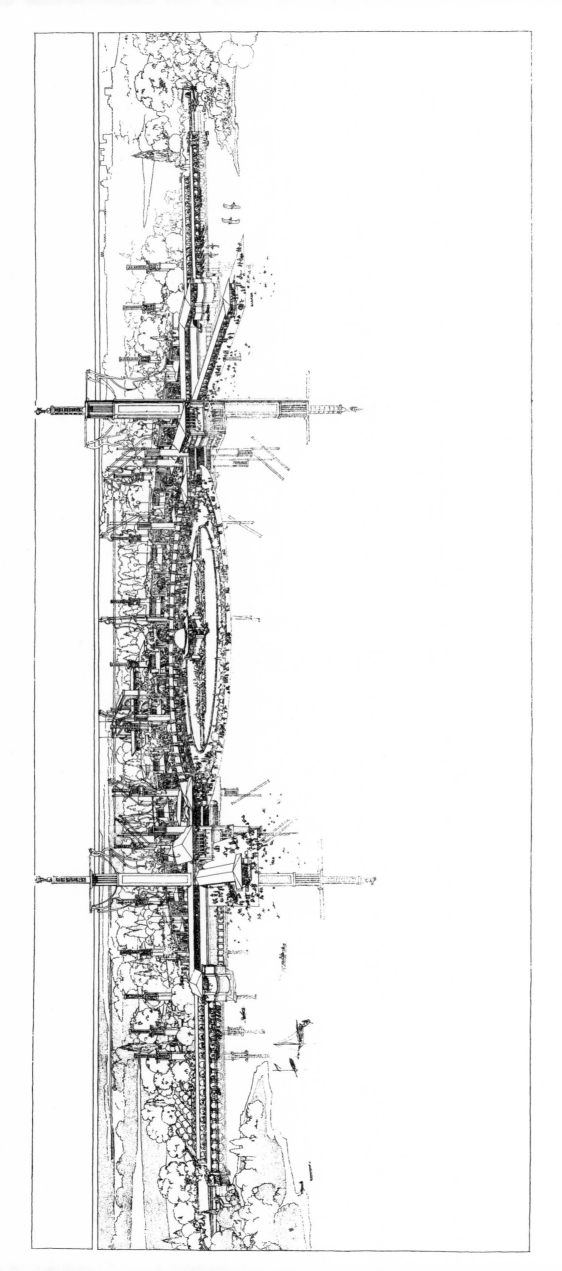

PLATE LX(a). Amusement resort designed to be built at Wolf Lake, Ind.

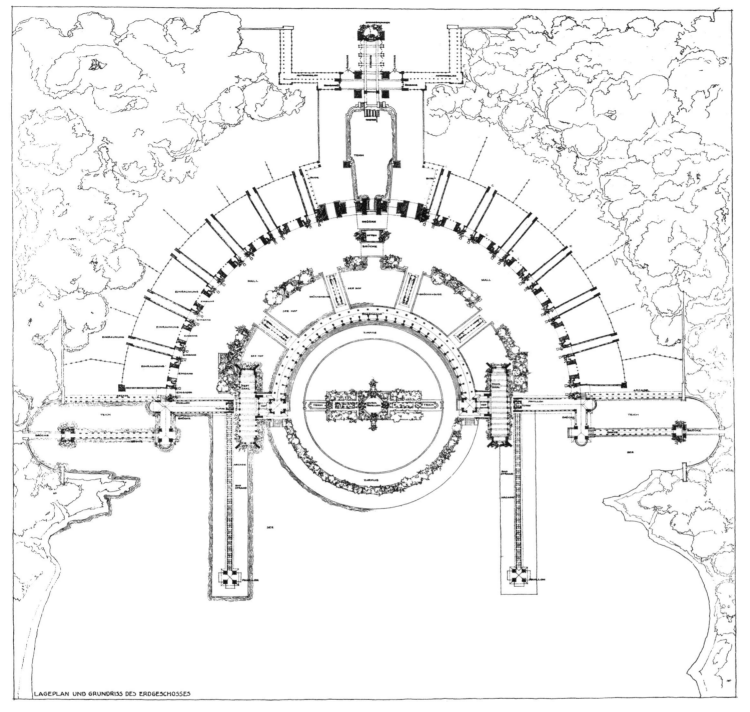

LAGEPLAN UND GRUNDRISS DES ERDGESCHOSSES

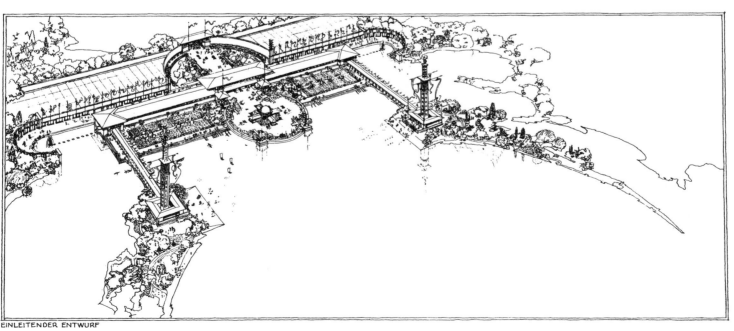

EINLEITENDER ENTWURF

PLATE LX(b). Ground plan and study for amusement resort, Wolf Lake.

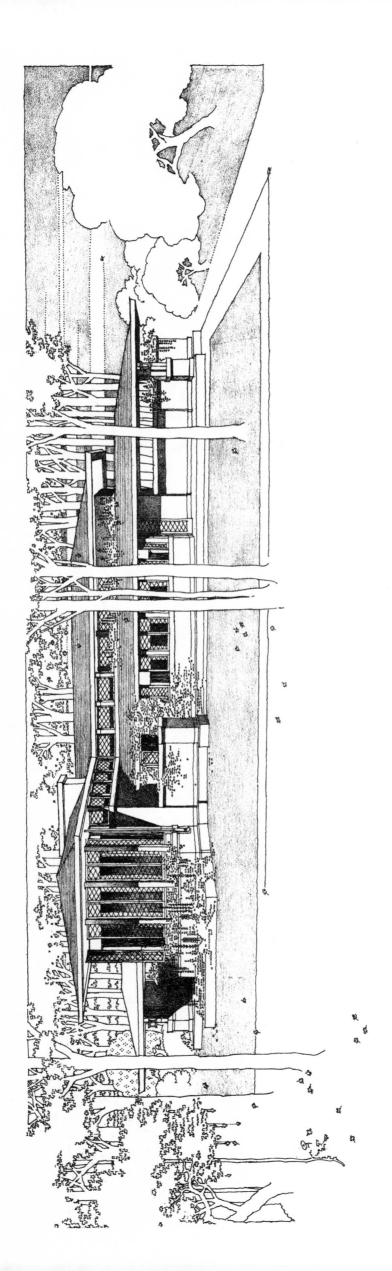

PLATE LXI. Dwelling for William Norman Guthrie, Sewanee, Tenn.

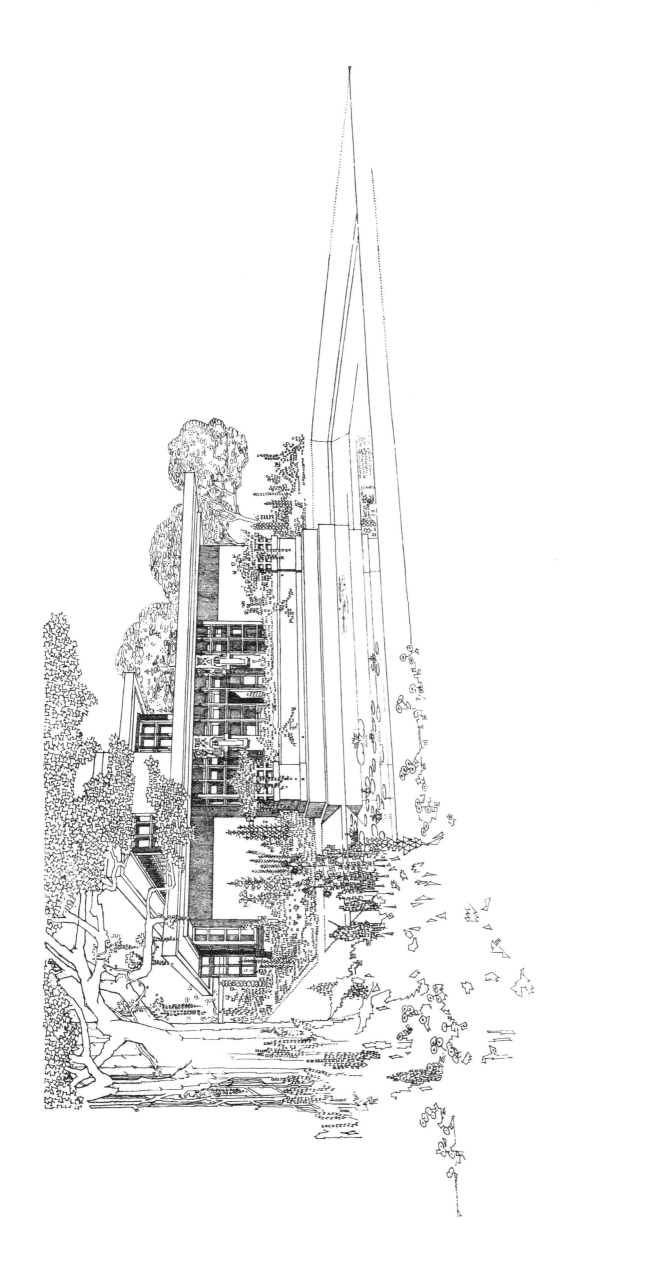

PLATE LXII(a). Atelier in concrete for Richard Bock, sculptor, Oak Park, Ill.

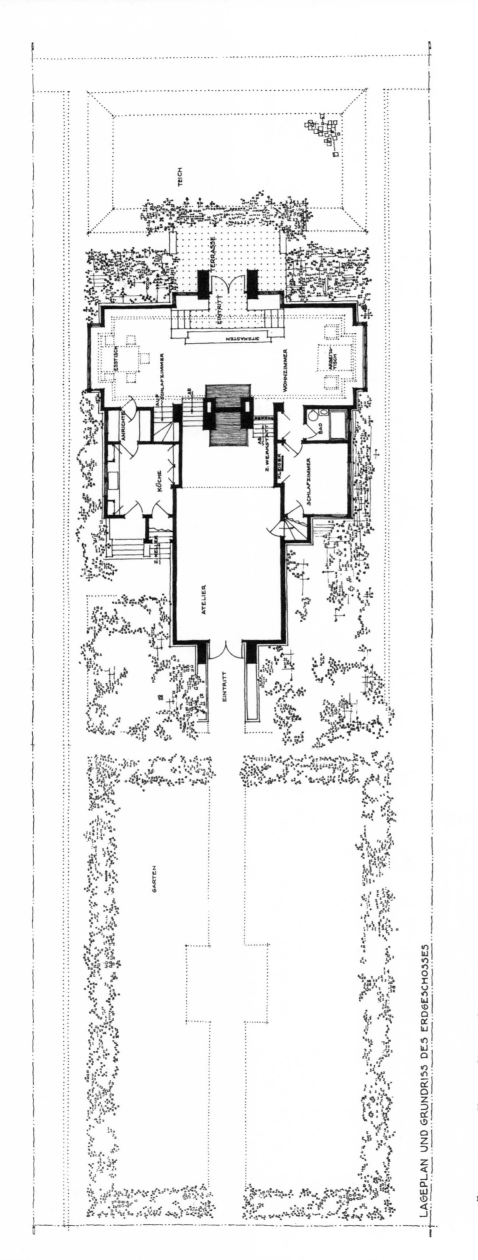

LAGEPLAN UND GRUNDRISS DES ERDGESCHOSSES

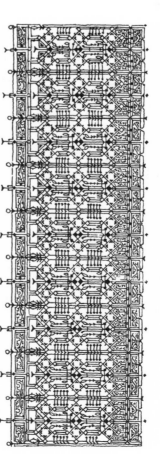

Plate LXII(b). Ground plan for the Bock atelier.

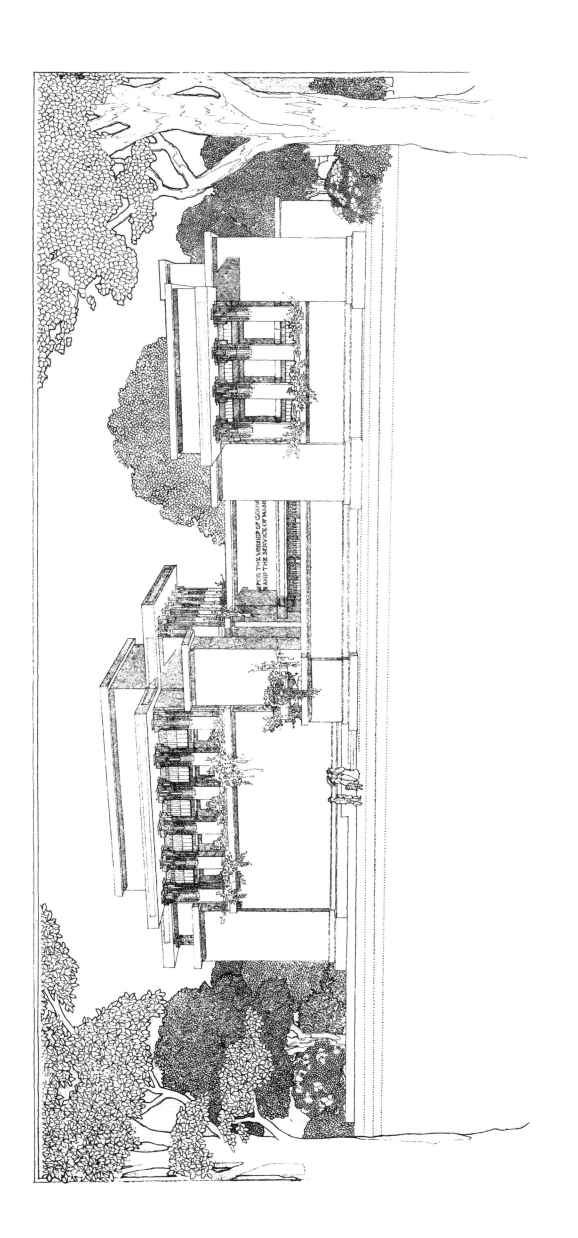

For the Worship of God and the Service of Man

PLATE LXIII(a). Design for house and temple, Unity Church, Oak Park, Ill.

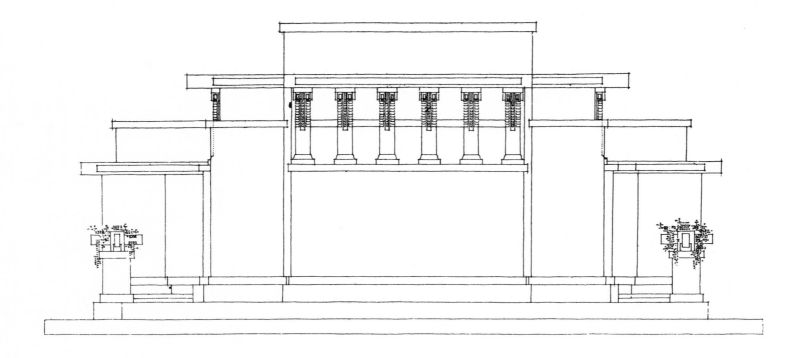

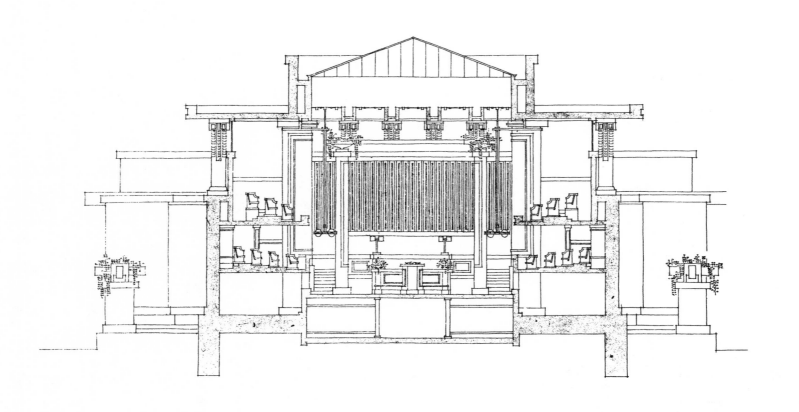

PLATE LXIII(b). Elevation and cross section of Unity Temple.

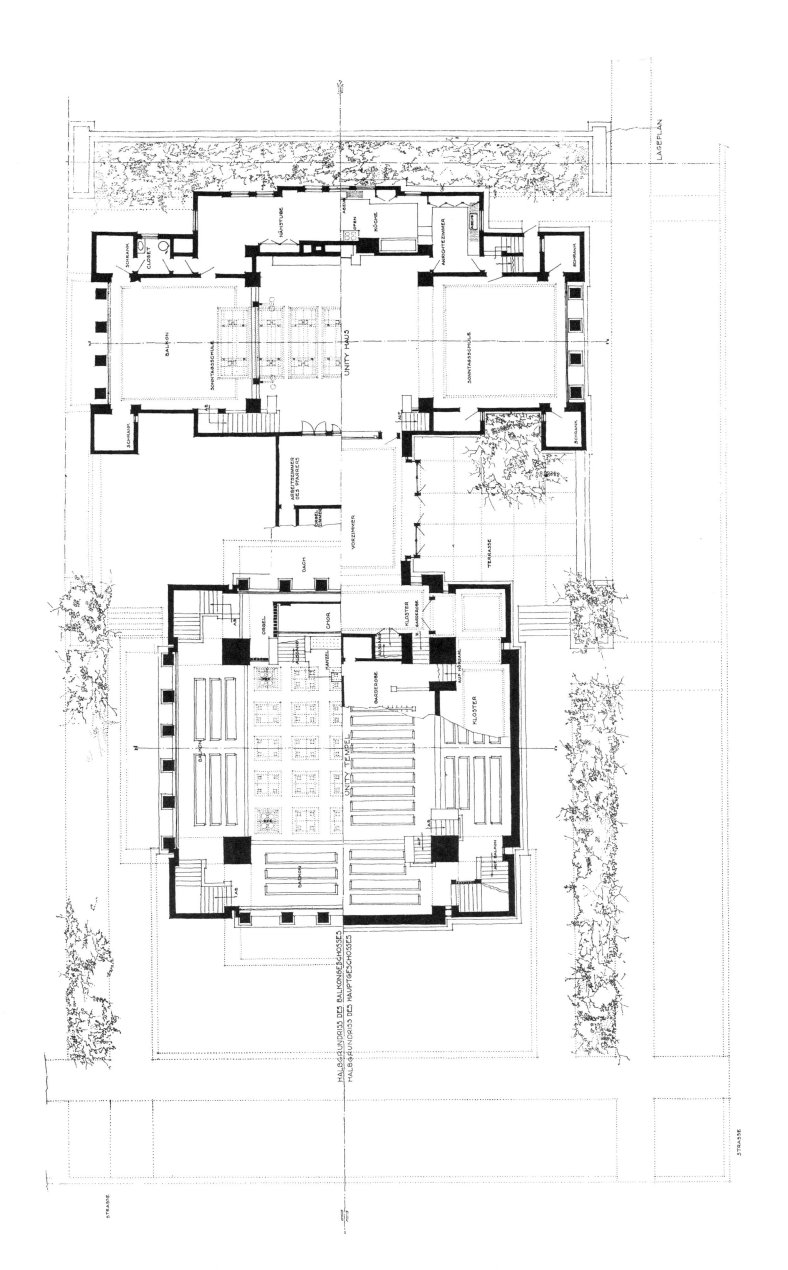

Plate LXIV(a). Ground plan, Unity Temple.

PLATE LXIV(b).   Facade of Unity Temple.